The Drama of Christianity

S. L. MORRIS, D.D., LL.D.

The Drama of Christianity

An Interpretation of the Book of Revelation

S. L. Morris

BAKER BOOK HOUSE
Grand Rapids, Michigan 49506

Paperback edition issued 1982 by
Baker Book House
from the 1928 edition of
the Presbyterian Committee of Publication

ISBN: 0-8010-6136-9

PHOTOLITHOPRINTED BY CUSHING - MALLOY, INC.
ANN ARBOR, MICHIGAN, UNITED STATES OF AMERICA

PREFACE

THE AVOWED PURPOSE of this study is an Interpretation of the Book of Revelation, otherwise known as the "Apocalypse"—its literal designation in the Greek being equivalent to an "unveiling." No studied attempt will be made either at *exegesis* or *exposition,* except incidentally in certain strategic texts, or distinct parts, which necessarily involve the question of interpretation.

Notwithstanding the name Apocalypse, literally translated, signifies an "unveiling," yet it is a "sealed" book to multitudes of earnest Bible students. It falls little short, seemingly, of irony in its professed object as an "unveiling," while as a matter of fact in its practical understanding by the church in all ages it is a *concealing.* The reason of this confusion of thought is due largely to the fact that many regard it as a prophetic revelation of the future, instead of an "unveiling" of the purpose of God in the Christian Dispensation.

The vast majority of devout people have nevertheless always received from individual texts, and detached portions, comfort in sorrow, resignation in trial and inspiration in life's conflicts, which have rendered it invaluable in the religious experiences of the saints in all the history of the church—perhaps a larger service than if they had been furnished instead merely a key to its interpretation. In other words, the lack of a full understanding of its scope has never interfered with its practical value to the child of God as an unfailing consolation in deepest distress. Nevertheless, it was written and intended for study, meditation and understanding. "Blessed is he that readeth and they that hear the words of this prophecy," is its initial promise.—Rev. 1:3. Equally significant is its closing threat against violating the integrity of its message.—Rev. 22:18, 19.

Among the Church Fathers Chrysostom makes no allusion to it. Luther undervalued it; and so did Calvin, chief of the Reformers, notwithstanding his voluminous commentaries of other Scripture. Was it Spinoza—or Immanuel Kant—who avowed that its author was a fit subject for the lunatic asylum? Each writer who offers a new interpretation is regarded with similar suspicion, and must first of all overcome the suggestion of presumption as guilty of "rushing in where angels fear to tread"—and where the greatest of Biblical scholars have confessedly failed.

Despite these unfavorable considerations, the author makes no apology for this contribution to the study of the Apocalyptic literature of the church. "Revelation," once the most confused and confusing to him of scriptural writings, is now a new book as clear as crystal. His confusion in the past was due largely to the fact that the Judgment Scene occurred seemingly in the wrong place—in the end of the sixth chapter and in several other unaccountable places, rather than appropriately at the end of the book. Instead, therefore, of meaningless, haphazard arrangement of its contents, the *Book of Revelation* is now to him a perfect unity, the most methodical and symmetrical of all the inspired writings. His interpretation doubtless will be compelled to run the gauntlet of possible rejection by reason of this very contention, that Revelation is the most perfect in conception and unique in its arrangement of any book written either by sacred or secular authors.

The first insight into its meaning was furnished by a hint of Professor William Milligan, of Aberdeen, Scotland, nearly forty years ago. In his treatise, "The Revelation of St. John," he suggested the thought that it consisted of a series of visions, each in the form of a panorama, not occurring in historic succession, but as repetitions of the same events in entirely new settings from different angles, each having a distinctive object in the various presentations. It was not entirely original with Milligan—being as a matter of fact centuries old—but interestingly and forcefully presented. Obligation to him is hereby acknowledged for the seed-thought, that developed in the mind of the author into a conception of its meaning, which he first published as a newspaper article in 1892 during his pastorate in Macon, Ga.

No apology is offered Professor Milligan for this adaptation of valuable material—much of it being common property

—which, however, will differ from him in important details. Many other authorities have aided this study, which call for no acknowledgment, but their contributions will appear as quotations.

This contribution to the difficult subject of Apocalyptic literature is given publicity, not as propaganda in the interests of any theory of the Millennium, but that others may be similarly benefited by this suggested key to a clearer understanding of the scope and purpose of the Apocalypse; or, at least, that they may be stimulated to further research as to "the mind of the Spirit" in its production.

"He that hath an ear let him hear what the Spirit saith unto the churches."

SAMUEL LESLIE MORRIS

ATLANTA, GEORGIA

CONTENTS

The PROLOGUE

TEXT: CHAPTER 1:1-8

John: "The Revelation of Jesus Christ, which God gave unto him, to shew unto his servants things which must shortly come to pass; and he sent and signified it by his angel unto his servant John: who bare record of the word of God, and of the testimony of Jesus Christ, and of all things that he saw.

"Blessed is he that readeth, and they that hear the words of this prophecy, and keep those things which are written therein: for the time is at hand."

John: "To the seven churches which are in Asia: Grace be unto you, and peace from Him which is, and which was, and which is to come; and from the seven Spirits which are before His throne; and from Jesus Christ who is the faithful witness and the first begotten of the dead, and the prince of the kings of the earth.

"Unto Him that loved us and washed us from our sins in His own blood, and hath made us kings and priests unto God and his Father; to Him be glory and dominion for ever and ever. Amen.

"Behold, He cometh with clouds; and every eye shall see Him, and they also which pierced Him: and all kindreds of the earth shall wail beause of Him. Even so, Amen."

Jesus: "I am Alpha and Omega, the beginning and the ending, saith the Lord which is, and which was, and which is to come, the Almighty."

CHAPTER I

CHARACTERISTIC FEATURES

TO JOHN, the beloved, the last surviving Apostle of the Twelve, was accorded the privilege of speaking the final word of inspiration—thereby closing the canon of Scripture. Biblical scholarship differs, however, as to whether the last book written was the Gospel of John, one of his Epistles, or the Apocalypse. In the practical use of the Bible it is of little consequence which of these was the last product of his pen—and therefore the closing word of inspiration. The providence of God, which determined the permanent arrangement of the books of Scripture in their order, has assigned to the Apocalypse the last place in the canon. This has the practical effect of making it the final message of God to a lost world.

Inspired Authorship

From Moses, author of the Pentateuch, to John many "Holy men of God spake as they were moved by the Holy Ghost," through a period of nearly fifteen hundred years. Profound scholars and the most illiterate, kings and peasants, poets, prophets and philosophers, wrought upon this masterpiece of the ages without collusion or conference, each with little or no thought of the others—nearly forty in all—and there is not the slightest conflict or contradiction from Genesis to Revelation; but instead, a unity of purpose binds the separate parts, like the robe of the Master "woven without seam throughout,"—the miracle of the ages.

Written in the solitude of the desert or in the heart of the crowded city, emanating from kings' palaces or from foul prisons, whispered in secret places or proclaimed on mountain tops—considered solely as literature—it is the sublimest of seraphic expression, the deepest of philosophic thought and the most practical and perfect of all moral codes.

Left alone, his companions having all fallen victims of tyrants, the executioner's axe or the fiery furnace, John, nearly one hundred years of age, formally closes the canon of Scripture; and the voice of Inspiration is hushed till the trumpet shall sound, which will summon a world to the grand assize for its final account.

Patmos

The date of its composition is somewhat uncertain. Whether this "Revelation," intended primarily for "the Seven Churches which are in Asia"—and ultimately for the church of God throughout the ages—was given in 67 A. D. or in 96 A. D. cannot now be determined. The historic place, however, is not left to conjecture. "The isle that is called Patmos," a barren rocky land of mountain ridges in the Mediterranean, enjoys its chief distinction as being the scene of John's banishment—"for the Word of God and for the testimony of Jesus Christ"—which event occurred during the reign of Nero about 67 A. D., or during the persecution of Domitian in 96 A. D. If written before the destruction of Jerusalem 70 A. D., that fact would throw light upon the interpretation of certain significant passages, serving perhaps as a warning to contemporary Christians; but this would in no way affect its meaning and message for the church of succeeding ages. It matters little to Christians of later periods, whether Nero or Domitian—if either—was primarily "the Beast" that symbolizes the spirit of world-kingdoms in their antagonistic attitude to the spiritual kingdom of Christ.

Its Place in Scripture

Each separate book in the canon has a sphere and distinctive place of its own. Genesis is the book of beginnings, the only authentic account of creation, and furnishes a brief compendium of the earth's earliest ages. The remaining books of the Old Testament record the history and experiences of the Jewish Nation. The Gospels contain the early life and ministry of Christ. The Acts of the Apostles is little else than a history of the church in the early days of Christianity. The Epistles of the New Testament narrate the history of Christian doctrine and expound its meaning.

Revelation is not simply a fitting close in its appropriate place as the last book in the canon of Scripture, but it serves as a spiritual rather than a historic program of Christianity itself. Distinctive historic books exhibit the track along which the church has traveled in the past. Prophetic writings reveal dimly the future course of its pilgrimage. The Book of Revelation deals alike with the past, present and future of the Christian Dispensation. Amid the fires of persecution and the fierce conflicts of the church militant, it guarantees assurance of future triumph—an inspiration in every age to disheartened, discouraged, suffering saints.

The Apocalypse approaches Moses in singing of the new deliverance, Isaiah in celebrating the glory of the church triumphant, and it surpasses all others in its description of the New Jerusalem with its pearly gates, its streets of gold and Paradise restored, with its "water of life, clear as crystal" and its tree of life which "bears twelve manner of fruits," whose "leaves are for the healing the nations."

In its distinctive characteristics it is unique. No other book in the entire Bible approaches its conspicuous features. It has an individuality peculiarly its own, pre-eminently striking, not simply in its organic structure, but as well in its internal composition, mystic symbols and spiritual significance.

1—*Comprehensive Epitome of Divine Truth*

The Apocalypse is an epitome of the whole Bible, a unique interweaving of all the symbols, types, shadows, figures and fundamental ideas of the entire Old Testament into one comprehensive book of brief compass. Just as the acorn contains in embryo and potentiality the entire oak with its roots, fibre, bark, branches and leaves, so Revelation as no other one book embodies in itself the entire volume of the Scriptures.

One cannot fully understand its meaning, significance, scope and design without the greatest familiarity with the

"Seraphim" of Isaiah, the "Cherubim" of Ezekiel, and the "Beasts" of Daniel, the "olive trees" of Zechariah, "Babylon" and the "New Jerusalem" of both Testaments, "the song of Moses and the Lamb," the "Elders" of the synagogue, the story of "Balaam" and of Jezebel," the "manna" of the wilderness, the "palms" of victory, the "plagues" of Egypt, the "trumpets" of Jewish worship, the "incense" of the tabernacle, etc. As a whole it is modeled after the apocalyptic writings of Ezekiel and Daniel. What Ezekiel and Daniel were to the Jewish Church, the Apocalypse is to the Christian. Jewish imagery and terms are baptized into a new significance and dedicated to the new task of expressing Christian thought and doctrine. It is New Testament thought and ideas expressed almost exclusively in Old Testament language and symbols.

2—Its Symbolic Form

Divine Revelation may take the form of authentic narrative, in which the finger of God may be vividly exhibited, and interpreted, as in the case of the handwriting on the wall, or left to the imagination and rational powers of the reader to search out its hidden meaning. It may, however, be cast in other forms—sublime poetic thought, didactic reasoning, prophetic foreclosure of future events and divine purposes; or in the imagery of mystic symbols, resembling and yet differing from allegory, parable and type. The Apocalypse belongs to the latter, presented in a series of mystic visions.

The natural and the spiritual are so closely related, the product of the same divine mind, that numerous objects in nature—fire and water, wind and hail, thunder and lightning, bread and wine, rocks and mountains, sun, moon and stars—are capable of conveying spiritual thought. Drummond's "Natural Law in the Spiritual World" is based upon the assumption that the two worlds are the counterpart of each other.

Symbolism abounds pre-eminently in the Scriptures, and was the favorite method of Christ himself for conveying to the minds of His disciples the most impressive spiritual truth as to His person, mission and relation to the individual believer and the church, saying, "I am the bread of life," "the door of the sheep," "the true vine," etc.

"In the Symbol," says Auberlen, "as well as in the parable, the lower is used as a picture and sign of the higher, the natural as a means of representing the spiritual. All nature becomes living: it is a revelation of God and of the divine mysteries and laws of life in a lower sphere, as much as the kingdom of heaven is in a higher. . . . It is on this correspondence that symbolism and parabolism are grounded. The selection of symbols and parables in Scripture therefore is not arbitrary, but is based on an insight into the essence of things. The woman could never represent the kingdom of the world, nor the beast the church. . . . To obtain an insight into the symbols and parables of Holy Scripture, nature, that second or rather first book of God, must be opened as well as the Bible." It is, therefore, in accordance with "the eternal fitness of things," that the judgments of God should be represented by thunder, lightning and hail, and His mercy by the rainbow. "White" is the natural symbol of purity; "red," the emblem of bloodthirstiness and war; and earthquakes, of mighty upheavals and convulsions.

In any rational interpretation of the Apocalypse there must be no confusion of terms. The same symbols must always be given the same meaning, and interpreted in strict accordance with symbolic language. The charactersitic quality of truth is its consistency. Any interpretation of a symbol which cannot apply uniformly is evidence that the reader has missed the way. The symbolic character of the Apocalypse is, therefore, its outstanding feature; and if that fact is not recognized, or is overlooked, the reader will wander hopelessly in the labyrinth of a mystic maze.

3—*Symbolic Numbers*

Its most striking peculiarity in this respect is its prevalent use of symbolic numbers—the number seven leading all the rest: Seven churches, seven stars, seven angels, seven golden candlesticks, seven seals, seven trumpets, seven thunders, seven vials with the seven last plagues, seven heads of the beast, seven mountains of the city, seven eyes of the Lamb, and seven Spirits before the throne.

As seven is divided almost equally by its components, three and four, so these two numbers play almost as conspicuous part as seven itself. There are four living creatures, four angels standing on the "four corners of the earth," holding in their hands the four winds; four angels are bound in the great river Euphrates, etc. Equally remarkable is the frequent occurrence of the number three. There are three woes, three unclean spirits like frogs, three parts into which Babylon is divided, three gates on each side of city which is foursquare. Even the very divisions of the sevens occur between the three and four parts. This may be verified by examining the message to the seven churches, the seven seals, seven trumpets, and seven vials of wrath, where there is always a noticeable change occurring between the three and four in each series. This could be abundantly illustrated but would extend the limits of this study beyond reasonable bounds and thereby divert the mind from the real purpose of the author. Other significant figures are "six hundred three score and six," the number of the beast, and "a thousand years," the basis of all Millennial literature.

4—*Characterized by Its Christology*

No book in all the Bible is so pervaded with the presence, personality, power and purpose of Christ. Not even the Gospels which contain the events of His earthly life are perhaps so complete a revelation of Himself. He appears as its chief personage, introduced in the first chapter as the author of Revelation and chief speaker, delivering the messages to the seven Churches, opening the seven seals of the Book, standing on Mt. Zion with the 144,000, leading the spiritual hosts to victory, the Judge on the great white throne, and as speaking the final word to the church and the world in the closing chapter. While it reveals Christ in His threefold office as Prophet, Priest, and King, the larger emphasis is given a different threefold aspect of His life and work as may be seen by the following:

(1)—Revelation is saturated with the thought of redemption by His blood. It opens with ascriptions of praise "unto him that loved us and washed us from our sins in his own blood." Everywhere on its pages the epithet most frequently given Him is "The Lamb," the symbol of atoning sacrifice. In the midst of the throne He is beheld, "a lamb as it had been slain." The redeemed are represented as having "washed their robes and made them white in the blood of the Lamb." It is said "the Lamb which is in the midst of the throne shall feed them and lead them unto living fountains of waters." This great multitude which "stood before the throne and before the Lamb . . . cried with a loud voice saying, Salvation to our God which sitteth on the throne and unto the Lamb." The victorious hosts are represented as "overcoming by the blood of the Lamb." The redeemed church is "the bride, the Lamb's wife." Their names are written in "The Lamb's book of life." The New Jersualem is described as having no need of sun, "for the glory of God did lighten it and the Lamb is the light thereof"; and "the Lord God Almighty and the Lamb are the temple of it." The river of the water of life proceeds "out of the throne of God and of the Lamb."

(2)—The outstanding event of Revelation is the Second Coming of Christ. The great prophecy of the Old Testament is the First Coming of Christ. The great prophecy of the New Testament is the Second Coming. It has been computed that one verse in every eleven of the latter refers to it. No other book in the entire Bible is so pervaded with it as Revelation. It opens with the statement, "Behold he cometh with clouds." In five out of seven of the messages to the churches it is mentioned. The one voice in all the "seals," "trumpets" and "vials" is the statement, "He cometh." The nineteenth chapter contains a magnificent description of His coming:

"And I saw heaven opened, and behold a white horse; and

he that sat upon him was called Faithful and True, and in righteousness he doth judge and make war.

"His eyes were as a flame of fire, and on his head were many crowns; and he had a name written that no man knew but himself. And he was clothed with a vesture dipped in blood; and his name is called The Word of God. And the armies which were in heaven followed him upon white horses, clothed in fine linen, white and clean.

"And out of his mouth goeth a sharp sword, that *with it he* should smite the nations; and he shall rule them with a rod of iron: and he treadeth the winepress of the fierceness and wrath of Almighty God. And he had on his vesture and on his thigh a name written, King of Kings, and Lord of Lords."

The last chapter asserts three times: "'I come quickly," one of the three being the closing message of Scripture which evokes the fervent response, "Amen. Even so, come Lord Jesus,"—in which prayer every child of God joins most devoutly. It is the blessed hope of the church, the consummation of all the ages.

(3)—The third distinctive feature in the Christology of the Apocalypse is the "reign" of Christ. Multitudes of those, who love our Lord Jesus most loyally and devoutely, anticipate His reign as some *future* outstanding event, which shall crown His work and in which all enemies shall be put under His feet, when every knee shall bow and "every tongue shall confess that Jesus Christ is Lord to the glory of God the Father."

These fond hopes will be fully and gloriously realized. In their longing, however, for this consummation they lose sight of the fact that Jesus is *already on the throne* of the heavens. Whatever the future may have for Him, both the Scriptures and the Creed assert: "He sitteth at the right hand of the Father." The great Commission investing the church with the responsibility of world-conquest proceeds upon the basis that He is already on the throne, now reigning, and His guiding hand is not impotent: "All power is given unto me in heaven and in earth . . . And, lo, I am with you always, even unto the end of the world." The Book of Revelation furnishes the comforting assurance of His present reign embodied in the hymnology of the church, the following being a specimen:

"Hark! ten thousand harps and voices
Sound the note of praise above:
Jesus reigns, and heaven rejoices:
Jesus reigns, the God of love:
See, he sits on yonder throne,
Jesus rules the world alone."

The reign of Christ is the guarantee that history is not the result of chance. Revelation is the "unveiling," the lifting of the curtain, showing His divine guiding and ruling hand, bringing to pass the events of history according to a definite pre-arranged plan.

If faith staggers in its weakness, or gropes in the darkness, Revelation lifts the curtain and exhibits the intimate connection between the things of heaven and earth, demonstrating that the events of earth are directed from the throne. Waves of purposes are revealed as starting in heaven which break on the shores to time. See Rev. 8:5 where fire from the altar in the heavenly realm, "cast upon earth," was accompanied by startling results in the earthly sphere. One of our poets has given an interpretation of providence, which might have been inspired by a glimpse behind the curtain such as John saw in the Apocalypse:

"History's pages but record
One death-grapple in the darkness
Twixt false systems and the Word.
Truth forever on the scaffold,
Wrong forever on the throne:
But that scaffold sways the future,
For behind the dim unknown
Standeth God within the shadow
Keeping watch above his own."

The same Christ on the throne, whose omnipotent hand guides the world in their orbits, takes notice of the fall of a sparrow and numbers even the hairs of the head of the saints.

The destiny of nations, the rise and fall of empires, are not more the object of His solicitude and providential oversight than the most insignificant event in the life of His humblest servant.

5—*Eschatology*

The last characteristic of the Apocalypse, calling for notice is its "Eschatology"—signifying a discourse of the "last things." It is the one book of Scripture which more than all others reveals the things pertaining to the end of the Dispensation, the future destiny of the righteous and the wicked, and gives a brief, faint flashlight of the dim unknown, designated as Eternity. As these future events catalogued under the theological term, Eschatology, will come up for consideration again and again in this study, no other notice will be given them here except their enumeration in the supposed order of their occurrence: 1—Unfulfilled Prophecy; 2—The Second Coming; 3—The Resurrection; 4—The Millennium; 5—The Last Judgment; 6—Heaven and Hell; 7—Eternity.

As a summary, the things discussed in this chapter, which characterize and make it distinctive from other inspired writings, are hereby rehearsed for convenient reference: 1—An Epitome of the whole Bible—with New Testament thought couched in Old Testament terms. 2—Its Symbolic Form. 3—The largest use of Symbolic Numbers. 4—Its exalted Christology. 5—Its Eschatology.

PURPOSE

TEXT: CHAPTER 1:9-20

John: "I, John, who also am your brother, and companion in tribulation, and in the Kingdom, and patience of Jesus Christ, was in the isle that is called Patmos, for the word of God, and for the testimony of Jesus Christ. I was in the Spirit on the Lord's day, and heard behind me a great voice, as of a trumpet, saying:

Jesus: "I am Alpha and Omega, the first and the last: and, what thou seest, write in a book, and send it unto the seven churches which are in Asia; unto Ephesus, and unto Smyrna, and unto Pergamos, and unto Thyatira, and unto Sardis, and unto Philadelphia and unto Laodicea."

John: "And I turned to see the voice that spake with me. And being turned, I saw seven golden candlesticks; and in the midst of the seven candlesticks one like unto the Son of man, clothed with a garment down to the foot, and girt about the paps with a golden girdle. . . .

"And when I saw him, I fell at his feet as dead. And he laid his right hand upon me saying:

Jesus: "Fear not; I am the first and the last: I am he that liveth, and was dead; and, behold, I am alive for evermore, Amen; and have the keys of hell and of death. Write the things which thou hast seen, and the things which are, and the things which shall be hereafter; the mystery of the seven stars which thous sawest in my right hand, and the seven golden candlesticks. The seven stars are the angels of the seven churches; and the seven candlesticks which thou sawest are the seven churches."

CHAPTER II

ITS STRUCTURE, INTERPRETATION *and* PURPOSE

THE KEYNOTE to the interpretation of the Apocalypse is its unique structure. It partakes somewhat of the form of a Greek drama with various parts, its different actors and, at regular intervals, its chorus singing its heavenly anthems, in which more specifically is revealed its spiritual purpose—Consolation.

Dramatic Form

It was written in the age of the Greek drama, a period characterized by the use of parables, pageants and panoramas. Sophocles, Euripides and Thucydides were masters in the use of the dramatic art for presenting their thoughts in a popular method to insure a hearing and acceptance by the common people. John may not have been familiar with these Classics; but in the school of Christ he had been taught, by means of parables, the use of the dramatic method in story form—which presented the concrete truth—for example, in the parable of the "prodigal," or in the character of "Dives," so strikingly, as to be living illustrations speaking through the ages. The age in which he lived, and the Spirit of God which inspired him, influenced John to write in simplest form the greatest drama in all human history, as will be seen by future study of his Revelation.

Dramas consist variously of prologue, parts, acts, scenes, interludes, choruses, plot and counterplot, temporary defeat and ultimate triumph of right—in which actors "have their exits and their entrances; and one man in his time plays many parts"—concluding often by the recitation of an Epilogue. All the required elements are contained in John's Apocalypse—the Drama of Christianity. The Dramatis Personae are God, Christ, Angels, Martyred Saints, Elders, the four Living Creatures, Satan, the Beast, the False Prophet, the Four Horsemen, Heavenly Choirs, and the Apostle John, both as actor and narrator. The scenes cover three worlds, Earth, Heaven and Hell. The acts consist of seven Panoramas. The period of time covers the entire Christian Dispensation. The Interlude with its significant chorus occurs regularly and unfailingly in each separate panorama.

THE INTERPRETATION

Various solutions of its significance and purpose have been attempted by as many types of Christian scholarship, but all may be included in four classes, mutually exclusive, according to the time-period assigned to the scope of its events. Any understanding of its message will be reached only by a careful consideration of each class and a discriminating elimination of those inconsistent with the facts of subsequent history, and the whole scope of its contents interpreted in the light of concurrent Scripture.

1—*Praeterists*

In the natural order, first must be considered the interpretation of the Praeterists. These are they who insist that the Book of Revelation deals almost exclusively with John's own age, the tribulations of the early Christians, and the destruction of Jerusalem. It was written, supposedly by this class, for the early Christians about A. D. 67, and intended as a warning of the approaching destruction of Jerusalem in the year 70 A. D. It largely exhausted its purpose, therefore, at the time and has no message for the church of the ages—except as lessons of past history and incidently as a type of the approaching end of the Christian Dispensation at the Second Coming.

Canon Farrar may be taken as a type of this class, and their interpretation is interestingly presented, backed by his eminent scholarship, in his thrilling story entitled, "The Early Days of Christianity." Accordingly the emperor Nero is the "Beast;" and to escape the consequences of the possible venting of his wrath on Christians for assigning him such a role, the information is conveyed under the cryptic number six hundred three score and six, which would be understood only by the initiated. To make this number apply to him, it is supposed that the Hebrew form, "Neron Caesar" is employed; and singularly enough, the letters according to the prevalent method of enumeration would total "six hundred three score and six." The Seventh Day Adventists, by ascribing a certain title to the Pope as "the Vicar of the Son of God," figure the numerals as "six hundred three score and six" proving, to their satisfaction, that he is "the Beast." Others have made this cryptic number apply to Napoleon Bonaparte. The fall of mystic Babylon was intended supposedly as the warning of the destruction of Jerusalem. The "three and a half years," "forty and two months," "twelve hundred and sixty days"—time equivalents—represented the exact length of the Jewish War under Vespasian.

It is needless to give further details, as this study is not intended as an elaborate discussion of theories of interpretation, nor for display of scholarship. Notwithstanding this interpretation brings to its support some scholarly men, it has never satisfied the thought of the church. It has many difficulties fatal to its acceptance. Supposedly written in 67 A. D. on an isolated island in the midst of the Mediterranean, only three years before the destruction of Jerusalem, it would have been utterly impossible to have accomplished the alleged purpose, since rapid transportation was lacking for its circulation. Even in that case, it would have served only a temporary purpose and have had no vital message for future generations.

2—*Historical Interpreters*

Next in order come the Historical Interpreters, who assert that the Book of Revelation is a complete record of the great outstanding events of Church History, continuously chronological, from the beginning to the glorious consummation at the end of the Dispensation. It has had its advocates for the past thousand years. Saintly and scholarly men as Dean Alford, Auberlen and, to a certain extent, Isaac Williams, have favored the historic interpretation. Some have applied the principle to the Kingdom of God, even extending it as far back as Creation, and have worked out a remarkably striking chronology, adapting it to the visions of the Apocalypse. The first eleven chapters would correspond to the Old Testament. The twelfth, beginning with "the woman travailing in birth" and bringing forth "a man child who was to rule all nations," would mark the beginning of the New Testament. The majority, however, confining the adaptation to the Christian Dispensation have attempted to find a parallel in the history of the church and the world.

Mohammedanism, the Papacy, the Saracens, the invasion of the Goths and Vandals, Luther and the Reformation, Napoleon and the French Revolution, have all been assigned places as fulfilment of the "woes," "judgments," "vials of wrath," "the fall of Babylon," etc. As a specimen of the historic method of interpretation Richard Frances Weymouth of England, cites—not, however, with approval—the following:

"The first six Trumpets embody the events that occurred after the great European revolution which broke out in 1793. The first received its fulfilment in the French Revolution; the second in the destruction of the fleets of France by such victories as those of the Nile, Cape St. Vincent, and Trafalgar; the third pointed to the desolation caused by the French wars throughout Europe; the fourth depicts the career of Napoleon 1; the fifth prefigures the humiliation inflicted by that great warrior upon the pope; while the sixth refers to the wasting away of the Turkish power. We are supposed to be living under the seventh plague now, and may almost at any moment expect the Second Coming and personal reign of our Lord."

Sixty years ago Dr. Cumming, of London, delivered a series of sensational lectures, adapting the visions of the Apocalypse to world-events, upon which he based a warning of the immediate end of the world, and which had more general acceptance and caused greater excitement than the Millerite Scare of 1842.

The historic method runs counter to the general plan of the structure of the Book, entirely overlooking the synchronism of its parts—which will be considered later—and would have ruthlessly robbed it of any real spiritual message for the church in all ages, and would have constituted it simply a puzzle-book for a guessing contest—as has been done by "freaks" and petty sects in the use of mistaken translations, strained interpretations, fanciful symbolisms and the irrational mixing of literal and figurative terms.

It has led to an arbitrary selection of historic "events" as proofs of the fulfilment of prophecy, each interpreter "doing that which was right in his own eyes," resulting in a recklessness of scriptural interpretation, paralleling the lawlessness of the days of the Judges. There has been as wide divergence among themselves, as there has been hopeless disagreement of professed scientists in their speculation concerning "spontaneous generation," evolution and other guesses based upon supposed scientific data. It has, moreover, compelled each speculative interpreter to revise his historical schedule to correspond to some new development of human history such as the World War, which has played havoc with his data, dates, "fulfilments" and personal prophecies of impending doom. Nothing daunted by their confessed failure, many of them immediately set about a reconstruction of their fallen house of cards. It brings bitter discouragements to their dupes, and breeds skepticism in many; while others make it the occasion of raillery and ridicule. Oliver Wendell Holmes, for example, gives birth to a humorous poem enumerating certain ludicrous "signs" which reaches the conclusion:

"Till then let Cumming blaze away,
And Miller's saints blow up the globe;
But when you see that blessed day,
Then order your ascension robe."

3—*The Futurists*

Closely akin to this continuously historic method, and equally as objectionable, is the Futurist School of interpreters. According to their conception the Apocalypse has practically but one message, and was written to forecast one conspicuous event, the Second Coming of Christ. All heresies and erroneous views of Scripture have ordinarily an element of truth as a basis. The Second Coming of Christ is the one great outstanding event of the future, the blessed hope of the church; but it may be so exclusively emphasized as to lead to wild fanaticism. Corn ground into meal is most nourishing food, but if one element is extracted to the exclusion of the rest, it may be manufactured into alcohol which produces intoxication—the counterpart of fanaticism.

This method has led very many of the saintliest men far afield, and has resulted in the extravagances of extreme Premillennialists who have ventured by calculations and "signs of the times" to fix the date of the Second Coming. Compelled to revise their figures and dates, they have discredited themselves and given occasion to modern scoffers to revive the skepticism of the past by raising the inquiry: "Where is the promise of his coming, for since the fathers fell asleep all things continue as they were from the beginning of the creation." Christian men might well consider whether their position is not of somewhat doubtful security, standing on the same platform with Millerites, Seventh Day Adventists, Russellites and other questionable interpreters of the inspired Word.

All Christians should regard the Second Coming as always imminent, and fervently unite in the prayer, Come, Lord Jesus, come quickly. Each should contribute to the hastening of the coming of the King and the extension of the Kingdom by preaching the Gospel "among all nations," but bitter controversies over human conceptions of a future divine event are not calculated to hasten its fulfilment. Surely the Book of Revelation was not intended to serve the sole purpose of agitating the mind of the church in each succeeding age as to whether "the signs of the times" indicated that the end of all things was immediately at hand. The Futurists admittedly hold the truth—but a half truth.

4—*Synchronists.*

The views of the Praeterists, Historicals and Futurists having alike failed to satisfy the church and to meet the facts of the case, there remains to be considered the interpretation of the Synchronists. Theirs is a spiritual conception as to the purpose of the Apocalypse, designed to deal not with events primarily but with eternal principles of the Kingdom. The Apocalypse is a series of panoramas in the form of visions, successive in presentation but not in consecutive historic relation. Each panorama covers the entire period of the Christian Dispensation. The Book is divided into seven cycles, each covering the same period and presenting each time a different phase of the Christian Dispensation.

It is the Drama of Christianity

A striking illustration of this method of successively presenting the same event, taken from classic literature, is Browning's poem, "The Ring and the Book." A murder having been committed, Browning conceives the idea of having it presented independently twelve different times. Each narrator deals with the same event, but each adds a new phase of the case. The whole truth is obtained by a composite conception of the twelve recitations. In like manner, the Apocalypse presents the Christian Dispensation in seven panoramas, each somewhat different from the other six. It would have been impossible to represent all the phases of Christianity in one panorama; but the reader must recognize the fact that they are synchronous—taking place often simultaneously—

and thereby obtain a composite conception, herein designated, "The Drama of Christianity."

Analogy of Scripture

This same method is pursued elsewhere in Scripture, and rather frequently. Joseph's dreams, as well as Pharaoh's, are doubled but each represents the same thought—"the dream is one." Still more striking is Nebuchadnezzar's dream of the "image"—interpreted by Daniel to signify coming World-Kingdoms succeeded by the Spiritual Kingdom "that shall never be destroyed." The identical revelation is contained in the seventh chapter of Daniel under the similitude of "Beasts"—World-Kingdoms succeeding each other until the time arrives when "the saints possess the Kingdom."

Christ himself pursues the same method in the thirteenth chapter of Matthew, where the Kingdom of heaven is represented again and again in separate parables, each presenting a different phase, but the whole truth must be gathered from this composite conception. For example, the parable of the "Mustard Seed" represents the outward development of the Kingdom; and the "leaven," its inward transformation—taking place at the same time. The "tares" and the dragnet add other features of the same Kingdom.

Modeled After Christ's Last Sermon?

The most striking and original contribution made by Prof. Milligan to the subject is his statement—sustained by argument of unusual ability—that the Apocalypse is modeled after Christ's Sermon on the Mount of Olives, recorded in the twenty-fourth chapter of Matthew. The resemblance is remarkably striking, as outlined by this scholarly interpreter; but may not the parallel between the two be due perhaps to the fact that both deal with the same period—the Christian Dispensation—and both pursue the same method of repeating the presentation under different phases? It is singular, perhaps significant, that John does not record Christ's last discourse. Is the Apocalypse his version of it, presented in the form of visions? Christ is as truly the author of the Apocalypse as of the Sermon on the Mount of Olives, and both undoubtedly deal with the same subject, though widely separated in the point of time.

The question of the disciples on the Mount of Olives as to "the sign of thy coming, and of the end of the world," indicates confusion of thought, identifying the two events as synonymous: and the subject is still further obscured by our English translation, "the end of the world," which should be rendered, "the end of the age." Confusion lingers to this day in the mind of the church by not recognizing the fact that "the end" may at times refer to the close of the Jewish Dispensation and at other times to the Christian age—designated occasionally "the world to come." In one sense "the end" applies to the whole Christian Dispensation. All previous ages had been preparatory. The present is "the consummation of the ages," the final act of the world-drama, affecting the destiny of the human race; and the author of the Apocalypse in his epistle so uses the term, saying, "Little children, it is *the last time*"—1 John 2:18. Christ answers the inquiry with certain observations and concludes in the fourteenth verse with the statement: "And this gospel of the Kingdom shall be preached in all the world for a witness unto all nations; *and then shall the end come.*" Having presented certain phases of the Kingdom reaching unto "the end," Christ immediately takes up again the Christian Dispensation under a new aspect and traces it again to the end of the age in verse twenty-seven: "As the lightning cometh out of the east and shineth even unto west; so shall also the coming of the Son of man be."

Having the second time reached "the end," he proceeds again to present certain aspects of the Dispensation by "signs" and carries the thought forward to "the Son of man coming in the clouds of heaven with power and great glory: And he shall send his angels with a great sound of a trumpet and they shall gather together his elect from the four winds, from one end of heaven to the other." If Christ presents the Dispensation again and again in its various aspects, why should not John pursue the same plan in his "Revelation?" If not modeled after the Sermon on the Mount of Olives, as Milligan contends, John at least has pre-eminent precedent for his method in the treatment of the subject.

Comparison of Its Parts

Hitherto the suggestion that the Apocalypse consists of seven panoramas, representing the Christian Dispensation under various aspects, has been argued from analogy and re-enforced by apt illustrations, now the time has come for examining more minutely these panoramas, or visions, in order to demonstrate this fact by a comparison of their common constituent elements. For purposes of comparison an analysis of the Book is hereby given, showing the seven Panoramas or Cycles; each, however, covering the same period:

1—THE FIRST CYCLE (*Chapters I-V*) "The Seven Churches," presenting Types of Spiritual Life.
2—THE SECOND CYCLE (*Chapters VI and VII*) "The Seals," exhibiting the Agencies employed.
3—THE THIRD CYCLE (*Chapters VIII-XI*) "The Trumpets," pronouncing Judgments upon the world.
4—THE FOURTH CYCLE (*Chapters XII-XIV*) "The Dragon" and the two "Beasts," revealing the Trinity of Evil.
5—THE FIFTH CYCLE (*Chapters XV-XVI*) "The Vials," presenting the Judgments upon Apostacy and False Faiths.
6—THE SIXTH CYCLE (*Chapters XVII-XIX*) "Babylon" and "the False Prophet," furnishing a graphic description of the End of the Age.
7—THE SEVENTH CYCLE (*Chapters XX-XXII*) "The Thousand Years," revealing the Doom of Satan and the Judgment of the Ungodly.

Each vision has its significant Interlude of consolation with its chorus, singing its paeans of victory and the triumph of righteousness.

That each vision, or cycle, covers the entire Christian Dispensation may be sufficiently shown by the fact that each ends with the coming of Christ or the Judgment Scene. The first ends (Rev. 3:20-21) with Christ standing at the door and the joint reign of Himself and saints. The second ends (Rev. 6:16-17) with a vision of the Judge "on the throne" and "the great day of his wrath." The third ends (Rev. 11:15-19) with "the kingdoms of the world are become the Kingdoms of our Lord and of his Christ;" and "thy wrath is come and the time of the dead that they should be judged." The fourth reaches the same scene (Rev. 14-14-20), "Behold, a white cloud and upon the cloud one sat like unto the Son of man, and the angel thrust in his sickle into the earth and gathered the vine of the earth and cast it into the great winepress of the wrath of God." The fifth carries forward to the same event (Rev. 16:17-21) and reveals "the cup of the wine of the fierceness of his wrath. And every island fled away and the mountains were not found." The sixth cycle ends (Rev. 19:11-21) with a description of the Second Coming and the last great conflict in which the forces of evil are overwhelmingly and finally defeated and cast into the "lake of fire burning with brimstone." The seventh and last cycle ends (Rev. 20:7-15) with Armageddon, the great white throne and the General Judgment.

The recurrence of this Judgment Scene with unfailing regularity at various intervals seven different times cannot be accounted for upon any other theory than the suggested explanation—visions of the present Dispensation presented again and again. Any other conception introduces confusion which accounts for the difficulties always encountered in the effort to reach an understanding of this symbolic book. Always it must be borne in mind that each separate panorama must not be considered entirely alone but a component part of all the others.

As the sun rises in the east and casts its rays of light on the distant mountain range in the west, there is a blending together of the whole seemingly into one vast range. As the sun mounts to the horizon and descends toward the west, its rays light up the intervening valleys, revealing the fact that it consists of several elevations. While each may be viewed separately, yet they are each and all parts of one great constituent whole. In like manner as we view the distant future by means of these separate visions of Revelation, in one case the outstanding event may be the Second Coming; another may exhibit the final Armageddon of the great spiritual conflict; and still another may reveal the great white throne and the General Judgment; yet they are all parts of the one supreme cataclysm with which the Dispensation ends. In answering the question of the Disciples as to "the end of the age," Christ uses the destruction of Jerusalem, with which the Jewish Dispensation closes, as a type and shadow of the universal collapse of the entire world-system with which the Christian Dispensation will terminate and eternity begin. That is the message and meaning of Revelation—the Drama of Christianity.

THE PURPOSE OF THE APOCALYPSE

Notwithstanding Christians in all ages have derived great spiritual benefit from it and been thrilled with its blessed visions of God and heaven, yet multitudes fail to get its one great distinct message. Its principal—almost its sole—purpose is *Consolation* in the awful agony of the church's fierce spiritual conflict.

Prosperity was the blessing of the Old Testament, promised to the obedient. It was the promise made to the Jewish Nation—the church in its infancy. See the twenty-eighth Chapter of Deuteronomy with its blessings pronounced upon the obedient and its curses upon disobedience—and the corresponding promises of the Ninety-first Psalm. Many a child of God reads the Old Testament promises to the obedient, and has his faith severely tested as he finds instead of prosperity, that he is called to pass through "the deep waters" of sorrow and conflict. The blessing of the New Testament is *adversity*. The Christian Dispensation witnesses the church promoted to a higher plane than worldly prosperity and honored with a participation in the sufferings of Christ; and it triumphs by means of the cross. The New Testament is filled with warnings that victory is only through "much tribulation."—"If we suffer, we shall also reign with him." The early Church was baptized with blood—being always in the fire of persecution. The Laodicean experience of ease, riches, etc., is always dangerous, because foreign to the purpose of God for the development of the highest type of character after the pattern of Christ, and by way of the cross.

Forewarned

The object of the Apocalypse is to prepare the church to expect spiritual conflict, the judgment of God upon an ungodly world and as well upon an apostate unfaithful church. At the same time, the church is not left to face its terrific conflict and its dark hours of agony without assurance of triumph and "a crown of glory" as an adequate compensation. However dark the cloud, Revelation always exhibits the silver lining. During the entire Christian Dispensation her mission is that of "the Church Militant;" but the abounding comfort assures always that she will be "the Church Triumphant," sharing the glory of her Lord.

The Chorus of Consolation

The one great lesson to be learned is, that while each cycle reveals judgments, woes, etc., yet each has its own distinct "Interlude," introducing its heavenly chorus. The whole point of this interpretation will be lost, unless it be kept clearly and tenaciously in mind that the object of the chorus is *Consolation.* In each separate cycle the chorus is always sung by heavenly voices. The conflicts, trials and woes are earthly—"upon the inhabitants of the earth"—but its chorus in heaven always sings of triumph, blessedness and glory. The object is to sustain the faith of the church in the midst of the fiery furnace of affliction and during the fierceness of the fight.

In heaven the martyred saints are crying "How long, O Lord," and the sufferers of earth are urged to await patiently the purposes of God for their complete vindication and final deliverance. The saints on earth are still in the midst of the conflict; and lest their faith fail, they are permitted to hear the chorus singing its Consolation—"Choir Invisible," but not inaudible. The music of heaven assures that "Servants" of the present dispensation will be "Kings" in glory. Martyrs shall be given crowns. "The sufferings of this present time are not worthy to be compared with the glory which shall be revealed in us."

The Keynote of the Apocalypse

The sections herein designated "Interludes" are by others —Dr Scofield for example—labeled "parenthetical," as if they were just thrown in, being of minor importance in the purpose of the Book. On the contrary, they are the keynote to its whole meaning. Leave them out, and it is one of the most distressing portions of Scripture with little left except "woes," "judgments," "earthquakes," "wars," "pestilences," etc. Take account of them, and they offset the darker calamities revealed as inevitable. They are the silver lining of the dark cloud of divine wrath. They are heaven's message in song—what the Psalmist terms "songs in the night." They reveal the love of God amid all these "woes," the consolation of "the God of all comfort."

Keep always in mind this thought, and the purpose of the Apocalypse will be "unveiled" more and more in the "chorus" of each Interlude, in the further study of this Drama of Christianity.

The FIRST CYCLE

TEXT: CHAPTERS II-V

Jesus: "Unto the angel of the church of Ephesus write; These things saith he that holdeth the seven stars in his right hand, who walketh in the midst of the seven golden candlesticks;

"I know thy works, and thy labour, and thy patience, and how thou canst not bear them which are evil: and thou hast tried them which say they are apostles, and are not, and hast found them liars: And hast borne, and hast patience and for my name's sake hast laboured, and hast not fainted.

"Nevertheless I have somewhat against thee, because thou hast left thy first love. Remember therefore from whence thou art fallen, and repent, and do the first works; or else I will come unto thee quickly, and will remove thy candlestick out of his place, except thou repent. But this thou hast, that thou hatest the deeds of the Nicolaitanes, which I also hate.

"He that hath an ear, let him hear what the Spirit saith unto the churches; To him that overcometh will I give to eat of the tree of life, which is in the midst of the paradise of God." . . .

Jesus: "And unto the angel of the church of the Laodiceans write; These things saith the Amen, the faithful and true witness, the beginning of the creation of God; I know thy works, that thou art neither cold nor hot: I would thou wert cold or hot. So then because thou art lukewarm, and neither cold nor hot, I will spew thee out of my mouth. . . .

"Behold, I stand at the door, and knock: if any man hear my voice, and open the door I will come in to him, and will sup with him, and he with me. To him that overcometh will I grant to sit with me in my throne, even as I also overcame, and am set down with my Father in his throne. He that hath an ear, let him hear what the Spirit saith unto the churches."

John: "After this I looked, and, behold, a door was opened in heaven . . . and, behold, a throne was set in heaven, and one sat on the throne. And he that sat was to look upon like a jasper and a sardine stone: and there was a rainbow round about the throne, in sight like unto an emerald. And round about the throne were four and twenty seats: and upon the seats I saw four and twenty elders sitting, clothed in white raiment; and they had on their heads crowns of gold. . . .

"And before the throne there was a sea of glass like unto crystal; and in the midst of the throne, and round about the throne were four beasts full of eyes before and behind. And the first beast was like a lion, and the second beast like a calf, and the third beast had a face as a man, and the fourth beast was like a flying eagle. And the four beasts had each of them six wings about him; and they were full of eyes within: and they rest not day and night, saying,

The Four Beasts: (Cherubim): "Holy holy, holy, Lord God Almighty, which was, and is, and is to come."

John: "And when those beasts give glory and honour and thanks to him that sat on the throne, who liveth for ever and ever; The four and twenty elders fall down before him that sat on the throne, and worship him that liveth for ever and ever, and cast their crowns before the throne saying.

The Elders: "Thou art worthy, O Lord, to receive glory and honour and power; for thou hast created all things, and for thy pleasure they are and were created."

John: "And I saw in the right hand of him that sat on the throne a book written within and on the backside, sealed with seven seals. And I saw a strong angel proclaiming with a loud voice, Who is worthy to open the book, and to loose the seals thereof? And no man in heaven, nor in earth, neither under the earth, was able to open the book, neither to look thereon. "And I beheld, and, lo, in the midst of the throne and of the four beasts, and in the midst of the elders, stood a Lamb as it had been slain, having seven horns and seven eyes, which are the seven Spirits of God sent forth into all the earth. "And he came and took the book out of the right hand of him that sat upon the throne. And when he had taken the book, the four beasts and four and twenty elders fell down before the Lamb, having every one of them harps, and golden vials full of odours, which are the prayers of saints. And they sung a new song, saying,

The Four Beasts and Elders: "Thou art worthy to take the book, and to open the seals thereof: for thou wast slain, and hast redeemed us to God by thy blood out of every kindred, and tongue, and people, and nation; and hast made us unto our God kings and priests: and we shall reign on the earth."

John: "And I beheld, and I heard the voice of many angels round about the throne and the beasts and the elders; and the number of them was ten thousand times ten thousand, and thousands of thousands; saying with a loud voice,

Angelic Hosts: "Worthy is the Lamb that was slain to receive power, and riches, and wisdom, and strength, and honour, and glory, and blessing."

John: "And every creature which is in heaven, and on the earth, and under the earth and such as are in the sea, and all that are in them, heard I saying,

The Whole Creation: "Blessing and honour, and glory, and power, be unto him that sitteth upon the throne, and unto the Lamb for ever and ever."

John: "And the four beasts said, Amen. And the four and twenty elders fell down and worshipped him that liveth for ever and ever."

CHAPTER III

The SEVEN CHURCHES—TYPES *of* SPIRITUAL LIFE

IN this first Cycle the panoramic character of the vision is not so marked as in others, until the Interlude is introduced which contains the Chorus. The object seemingly is to use the Seven Churches of Asia as types of spiritual life. They were evidently real historic churches.

Ephesus, the ancient metropolis of that section, was the scene of stormy events and thrilling experiences in the life of Paul, making the nineteenth and twentieth chapters of Acts most interesting reading. This church enjoyed three years of the ministrations of Paul; and to it he addressed the Epistle to the Ephesians, one of the greatest products of his pen. It was at different times favored with the ministry of Timothy and of John himself—where according to Polycarp, he was buried. It was the meeting place of the great Ecumenical Council of Ephesus in 431 A. D., which condemned the heresy of Nestorianism.

The floor plan of the great theater is still intact, a natural amphitheater extending up the inclined hillside, rising tier upon tier, and capable of accommodating 25,000 people. Here Paul's companions were subjected to the threatened fury of the mob. The site of the Temple of Diana, one of the seven wonders of the world, and the ruins of the great church of St. John are still exhibited to tourists.

Smyrna, the church of "tribulation," enjoyed the ministry of Polycarp—perhaps "the angel of the church in Smyrna" —where he suffered martyrdom, and where his tomb high upon the side of Mt. Pagus above the city still guides the sailor in his approach to the harbor. It was the one church of the "seven," which survived the persecutions of Rome, the vicissitudes of war and the ravages of time, till destroyed by the onslaught of the Turk in 1922; and with its destruction perished the last vestige of organized Christianity in all Asia Minor.

Pergamos enjoyed the distinction of being the seat of Roman authority in that section, and in allusion to that fact is designated the place "where Satan's seat is." It possessed at one time a great library, and Mark Anthony is said to have given 200,000 of its volumes to Cleopatra for the famous collection at Alexandria; and they presumably perished in the burning of the library of Alexandria at the hand of the fanatical Moslems.

Thyatira, from a Biblical viewpoint, is chiefly famous as the native place of Lydia, the first Christian convert of Europe, "a seller of purple"—incidental evidence of the accuracy of scriptural narrative as Homer alludes to its red and purple dyeing as one of the characteristics of her native place.

Sardis was situated on the Pactolus, which "rolled down its golden sand," seat of the government of Croesus, richest of all the ancients, and where perhaps occurred the incident in the life of Solon, one of the seven wise men of Greece; but alas! the city is now as "dead" as its decadent church of the inspired narrative.

Philadelphia is but a memory, and the miserable village which marks the site of this city of "brotherly love" is doubtless but a travesty of its departed fame.

The site of Laodicea has been identified; and, singularly enough, the warm springs of Hierapolis—mentioned once in Scripture, Col. 4:13, in connection with Laodicea nearby—may have been intentionally and significantly used as the symbol of its spriitual life, "neither cold nor hot." Possibly somewhere among these ruins there lies buried the lost Epistle of Paul to Laodicea—Col. 4:16. If the spade of the excavator should ever bring it to light, the world's "best sellers" will be eclipsed; and the autograph of the Apostle Paul would be the most valuable article in existence—crown jewels being but baubles in comparison—a testimonial to the superlative worth of Christianity.

Their spiritual life was evidently not fictitious but is correctly diagnosed by "the searcher of hearts" who represents himself as "walking in the midst of the seven golden candlesticks." Colosse, one of the churches of Asia Minor, in close proximity to Laodicea, is not included, possibly because its spiritual life was not distinctly typical. In all probability the order of their arrangement was more or less arbitrary, in order to present these types in the successive order of their degeneration—with the exception of Philadelphia—from the more spiritual type to that of total apostacy. Alas! the candlesticks have one by one all been removed from their place! Mohammedanism is now supreme where Christianity once flourished.

Analysis

Carrying out its uniform policy in the use of the number Seven, the message to each church is itself distributed into seven elements. This may be illustrated by an analysis of Ephesus, the first: 1—The Salutation, "To the angel of the Church of Ephesus." 2—The Designation of the Speaker, "He that holdeth the seven stars in his right hand, who walketh in the midst of the Seven Golden Candlesticks." 3—Commendation, "I know thy works and thy labor and thy patience." 4—Condemnation, "Nevertheless I have somewhat against thee, because thou hast left thy first love." 5—Warning, "Remember therefore from whence thou art fallen and repent and do the first works; or else I will come unto thee quickly and will remove thy candlestick out of his place except thou repent." 6—Exhortation, "He that hath an ear, let him hear what the Spirit saith unto the churches." 7—Promise, "To him that overcometh will I give to eat of the tree of life which is in the midst of the paradise of God." The same general order and policy are pursued in each of the other cases.

The message in each case is "to the angel of the church," an expression which has been variously interpreted. The idea of guardian spirits is scriptural, but it is doubtful whether it applies to any except individuals; and more than questionable is the suggestion of guardian spirits for churches. The word "angel" signifies a "messenger," and the plain, obvious meaning is evidently the minister of the church—but no arbitrary interpretation is essential or affects the scope and purpose of the Book.

1—*Possibly Typical*

These Seven Churches in their various types of spiritual life doubtless have their counterpart throughout the present dispensation. Perhaps there is not a church in existence which would not naturally be classified in one of the seven types according to whether commendable, though possibly beginning to lose its first ardor; whether practically dead, having only "a name to live;" or whether lukewarm and in danger of repudiation by the Master in deep disgust. Extending the thought still further, these types may represent the spiritual life of individual Christians, and may be accepted by each as a personal message with a call to discriminating self-examination and consequent repentance, if drifting toward Laodicean indifference—the most culpable and dangerous of all spiritual types.

2—*Possibly Periods of History*

Do they represent distinct periods of Church History? Many worthy men have so maintained. According to their interpretation, Ephesus—highly commended for "thy labor and thy patience, and how thou canst not bear them that are vile, and thou hast tried them which say they are apostles and are not, and hast found them liars; and hast borne and hast patience, and for my sake hast labored and hast not fainted," yet beginning to manifest a tendency to drift from its "first love"—is typical of the first period.

(1) Ephesus, in that case, would represent the Apostolic age of the church characterized by its missionary zeal, its purity and its patience in suffering. Now, however, the apostles one by one have borne their testimony and gone to their reward. Only John is left, living in exile, and the primitive church is losing the ardor of its first love and conspicuous zeal. (2) Smyrna in "tribulation," "tried" in the fiery furnace, would represent the age of Persecution, overlapping the Apostolic age, and extending through the ten great persecutions until relief comes, when, in the person of Constantine, Christianity mounts the throne of the Caesars. (3) Pergamos, designated as the place "where Satan's seat is," in allusion, as already indicated, to the fact that it was the headquarters of the Roman government for the province of Asia, is condemned for holding "the doctrine of Balaam," indulging in spiritual "fornication" and holding "the doctrine of the Nicolaitanes," hateful to the Master—whatever it may have been. This would represent the age of prosperity, the church no longer persecuted but now established as the State Religion and in the grasp of deadly heresy, which waxes worse and worse as narrated in Church History. (4) Thyatira follows, and it is no longer Balaam compromising with evil as in the case of Pergamos, but "that woman Jezebel which calleth herself a prophetess" is revealed, with her disposition "to teach and to seduce" God's "servants." This represents unmistakably the beginning and working of the Apostacy, resulting in the "dark ages" of ignorance, superstition and unbridled lust. "Jezebel" is significant, a woman corrupting the church. In later cycles she appears as "the false prophet," and as the harlot "seated upon a scarlet colored beast." It is a striking description of the Apostacy of the church, whether so intended or not, in dealing with Thyatira. (5) Sardis is the natural and inevitable result—having a "name to live" but "dead." This is surely an appropriate description of the age it is supposed to represent as realized in the history of the Roman Catholic Church at the time of the Reformation. (6) Philadelphia comes as a great relief.

It is free from condemnation, has set before it "an open door" of opportunity and is given marvelous promises of divine favor and protection in "the hour of temptation, which shall come upon all the world to try them that dwell upon the earth." This is supposed to represent the great Protestant Reformation, and certainly comes at a most appropriate place in the program for the purpose. (7) Laodicea, last of all, has nothing whatever to merit divine favor and its spiritual life is so nauseating to the Master as to provoke His most intolerant indignation. Laodicea represents the end of the age, the present materialistic, modernistic, pretentious period, which indicates the time is ripe for judgment.

Logical and Natural Order

Whether these Seven Churches represent distinct periods of Church History is exceedingly uncertain, but there can be no questioning the fact that a divine arrangement is intentionally exhibited in their order. Laodicea placed last and corresponding so strikingly to other scriptural representations of the Apostacy, with which the present Dispensation is scheduled to end, is most significant. If compared with the closing events of the other cycles, it can scarcely fail to produce the impression that it was not accidental. This statement is sufficiently important to merit closer examination.

3—*The Laodicean Age*

Does Laodicea stand for the close of the Dispensation? An analysis and comparison of the events which are common to the other cycles, and with which the age uniformly ends, exhibit the following characteristic features: Apostacy, the Second Coming of Christ, the Marriage Supper of the Lamb and the joint Reign of Christ and the Saints.

(1) Apply the test of Apostacy. In his sermon on the Mount of Olives, describing the end and giving "the signs of the times," he mentions among other characteristic things, "The love of many will wax cold."—Matt. 24:11. In a dif-

ferent form he had previously hinted at the great Apostacy in his significant question, "Nevertheless when the Son of Man cometh, shall he find faith on the earth?"—Luke 18:8. The Apostle Paul insists "That day shall not come except there come *a falling away* first and that man of sin be revealed, the son of perdition."—II Thess. 2:3. In the later panoramas dealing with the end, John designates the apostate church as "Mystery, Babylon the Great, the Mother of harlots and abominations of the earth."—Rev. 17:5. In connection with the announcement, "The hour of his judgment is come," it is declared "Babylon is fallen, is fallen, that great city, because she made all nations drink of the wine of the wrath of her fornication."—Rev. 14:8. Laodicea's spiritual condition is described as "neither cold nor hot," "lukewarm," provoking the disgust of the Master, saying of herself, "I am rich and increased with goods and have need of nothing," at the moment the Master was saying pitifully, "Thou art wretched and miserable and poor, and blind and naked." Is there any more apt description of the Apostacy, characteristic of the end of the age?

(2) Apply the test of the Second Coming. That the Christian dispensation will end with the Second Coming is so universally scriptural and so unanimously accepted, surely it is unnecessary to argue the question or furnish scriptural proofs. In His messages to the Seven Churches, Christ mentions again and again the imminence of His Coming. To Ephesus and Pergamos each was said, "I come quickly." To Sardis, "I will come on thee as a thief"—unexpectedly. To Philadelphia, "Behold I come quickly;" but when He speaks to Laodicea Christ is *already* come—at the very door—"Behold I stand at the door and knock." Is it a mere coincidence that the Laodicean state represents Christ at the very door?

(3) Apply the test of the Marriage Supper. In a later vision of the close of the Dispensation in connection with the Second Coming, the voice of a great multitude is heard in exultant shout announcing "The marriage of the Lamb is

come and his wife hath made herself ready. Blessed are they which are called unto the Marriage Supper of the Lamb." Corresponding to this it was said to the faithful in Laodicea, "If any man hear my voice and open the door, I will come in unto him and will *sup* with him and he with me." Is this another mere coincidence?

(4) Apply the test of the joint Reign of Christ and His people. The Scriptures everywhere teach, and the saints in all ages agree, that the coming of Christ will be the triumphant reign of Christ and His people. Is there anything to correspond to this in Laodicea? Hear the promise of the Master: "To him that overcometh will I grant to *sit with me in my throne,* even as I also overcame and am set down with my Father in his throne." These "marks" of the "end" exhibited in the case of Laodicea are sufficient to indicate that the messages to the Seven Churches present a distinct phase of the Christian Dispensation, and that Laodicea marks the "end of the world" and justifies the designation of the last times as the "Laodicean Age." Are not the descriptions of Laodicea's spiritual state and the religious conditions of Christendom today strikingly identical? Are we living in the Laodicean Age?

4—*Interlude and Chorus*

Each cycle has its own "Interlude" containing the "chorus" of consolation. The interlude of this first panorama is contained in Chapters IV and V. The staging and setting for the chorus are elaborate, gorgeous and beyond the power of the imagination to visualize. The panorama exhibits "a throne set in heaven," the occupant "like a jasper and a sardine stone," suggestive of glory and might and dominion. "The rainbow round about the throne in sight like unto an emerald," suggests fidelity to the covenant promise. "Out of the throne proceeded lightnings and thunderings and voices," suggestive of majesty and awe. "Before the throne there was a sea of glass like unto crystal" signifying beauty and purity.

The Elders

"Round about the throne were four and twenty seats," occupied "by four and twenty elders sitting clothed in white raiment; and they had on their heads crowns of gold." The number is significant representing the twelve Patriarchs of the Old Testament and the twelve "Apostles of the Lamb." They are designated neither as patriarchs nor apostles but "Elders" —Presbyters in the Greek. They are seated upon thrones and their brows are encircled with crowns, suggestive of authority and rule. The vision reveals in heaven no bishops, archbishops, cardinals nor pope. Presbyters are the normal type of ecclesiastical rulers, both in the Old and New Testaments.

The Cherubim

"In the midst of the throne and round about the throne were four beasts"—"living creatures" in the Greek. Are these the "cherubim" described in the Vision of Ezekiel naming the identical creatures?

Consider carefully the following

PARALLEL

EZEKIEL

"Out of the midst thereof came the likeness of four living creatures . . . . And every one had four faces, and every one four wings. . . . Their wings joined one to another. . . . As for the likeness of their faces, they four had the face of a man, and the face of a lion on the right side; and they four had the face of an ox on the left side; they four also had the face of an eagle," etc.—EZEKIEL 1:5-10.

JOHN

"And before the throne was a sea of glass like unto crystal: and in the midst of the throne and round about the throne were four beasts, full of eyes before and behind. And the first beast was like a lion, and the second beast like a calf, and the third beast had the face of a man, and the fourth beast was like a flying eagle," etc.—REVELATION 4:6-7.

The similarity between the two accounts is very striking, and both are supposed to describe the Cherubim. The slight variations are to be accounted for by the different angles from which each narrator viewed them. Ezekiel saw the four faces of each as a composite being. John seems to have seen the face of each as if they were separate creatures, but does not thereby indicate that they may not have had other faces, making each a composite and facsimile of the others. The translation "beasts," (zoa) is most unfortunate and should be "living creatures" as in Ezekiel, since the Greek has a different word for "beasts" (tharia) introduced later in Revelation 12 and 13 and the chapters following. Compare these Cherubim with the Seraphim of Isaiah 6:1-6 for their remarkable similarity and equally striking contrasts.

The lion stands for strength, the calf (ox) for service, the man for intelligence and the flying eagle for swiftness—the combination representing the highest type of glorified creation. Read Romans 8:19-22 for further illuminating comment. Each is represented as having "six wings about him . . . and they rest not day and night saying, Holy, holy, holy, Lord God Almighty, which was, and is, and is to come"—almost the exact language of the "Seraphim" of Isaiah.

(1) *The First Chorus and Heavenly Choir*

After this graphic description of the staging in the Interlude, comes the first "chorus"—sung in glory and by heavenly choirs. The four living creatures give glory and honor and thanks to Him that sat on the throne who liveth for ever and ever. The four and twenty elders fall down before Him that sat on the throne and worship Him that liveth forever and ever and cast their crowns before the throne, saying:

> "Thou art worthy, O Lord,
> To receive glory and honor and power;
> For Thou hast created all things,
> And for Thy pleasure they are and were created."

This is the song of Creation, sung by heavenly voices, but as the representatives of God's created universe, symbolizing the glory of an emancipated universe. The chorus is always reassurance, heaven's consolation for the sorrows of earth. Read again Romans 8:19-22. The same thought is often sung by earthly choirs, though in a minor key:

> "Come ye disconsolate, where e'er ye languish,
> Come to the mercy seat fervently kneel.
> Here bring your wounded hearts, here tell your anguish,
> Earth has no sorrows that heaven cannot heal."

(2) *The Song of Redemption*

Having heard the song of Creation, the heavenly stage is again set for the next "chorus." The scene now represents a Lamb "in the midst of the throne," "as it has been slain," taking the book for the purpose of opening the seals; whereupon "The four and twenty elders fell down before the Lamb having everyone of them harps and golden vials full of odors, which are the prayers of saints. And they sung a new song, saying:

> "Thou art worthy,
> To take the book,
> And to open the seals thereof:
> For Thou wast slain
> And hast redeemed us to God by Thy blood,
> Out of every kindred and tongue and people and nation;
> And hast made us unto our God kings and priests
> And we shall reign on the earth."

This is the Song of Redemption, sung by these heavenly representatives of the redeemed of all the ages. It is being echoed by an increasing multitude of earth in passionate song and will be re-echoed in ever widening areas till it reaches every tribe and nation unto earth's utmost bounds, and fills the universe with the music of redeeming love.

(3) *Angelic Songs*

Though angels cannot sing of redemption from experience, yet they as "ministering spirits sent forth to minister for them who shall be heirs of salvation," are tremendously interested and are permitted to participate in the celebration of the victory of the Lamb and the redeemed host. "The number of them was ten thousand times ten thousand and thousands of thousands, saying with a loud voice:

> "Worthy is the Lamb that was slain
> To receive power and riches and wisdom and strength
> And honor and glory and blessing."

(4) *The Grand Anthem of the Universe*

This seven-fold ascription of praise to the Lamb is succeeded by the grand anthem of the universe. The first "chorus" begins with a limited number singing of Creation, followed by the Song of Redemption. The angelic hosts, innumerable, swell the majestic anthem which gathers strength and numbers till now the whole Creation takes up the triumphant strains and fills the limitless universe with one vast volume of adoring worship.

"And every creature which is in heaven and on the earth, and under the earth and such as are in the sea, and all that are in them heard I saying:

> "Blessing, and honor and glory and power
> Be unto Him that sitteth upon the throne
> And unto the Lamb forever and ever.

"And the four beasts said Amen. And the four and twenty elders fell down and worshiped him that liveth for ever and ever."

Summary

The Interlude of the first Cycle thus contains four choruses; and uniformly the purpose of the Apocalypse is revealed in the chorus. Heaven sings consolation to the suffering saints of earth. The first Cycle presents the Christian Dispensation under the form of Seven Churches; in the Ephesus-struggle to maintain its "first love"; in the Smyrna-"tribulation" of persecution; in the Pergamos-temptation to compromise with worldly conformity; in the Thyatira-conflict with the "Jezebel" of heresy; in the Sardis-"deadness" of spiritual life; in the Philadelphia-warfare for truth and righteousness; and ending in the Laodicean-age of Apostacy.

The earthly aspect of the Kingdom is always trial, conflict, martyrdom and the tendency to Apostacy—contrary to the prevailing theory of the triumph of righteousness. The design of the Apocalypse is to forewarn the church of its militant aspect in a series of panoramas, but lest it should be overwhelmed and utterly discouraged, always in each panorama there is the Interlude that allows the suffering saints to hear the heavenly aspect in the "chorus" which sings of ultimate victory and the blessed compensation for earth's sorrows. Therefore the first cycle introduces the chorus of the four living creatures, the four and twenty elders, innumerable angels and finally the vast universe singing; and their theme is one—the triumph and glory of the Lamb, in which the saints shall have a blissful participation, sharing His throne and glory unto the ages of the ages.

The SECOND CYCLE

TEXT: CHAPTERS VI-VII

John: "And I saw when the Lamb opened one of the seals, and I heard, as it were the noise of thunder, one of the four beasts saying, Come and see. And I saw, and behold, a white horse: and he that sat on him had a bow; and a crown was given unto him: and he went forth conquering, and to conquer.

"And when he had opened the second seal, I heard the second beast say, Come and see. And there went our another horse that was red: and power was given to him that sat thereon to take peace from the earth and that they should kill one another: and there was given unto him a great sword. . . .

"And when he had opened the fifth seal, I saw under the altar the souls of them that were slain for the word of God, and for the testimony which they held: and they cried with a loud voice, saying,

Martyrs: "How long, O Lord, holy and true, dost thou not judge and avenge our blood on them that dwell on the earth?"

John: "And white robes were given unto every one of them; and it was said unto them, that they should rest yet for a little season, until their fellowservants also and their brethren, that should be killed as they were, should be fulfilled.

"And I beheld when he had opened the sixth seal, and, lo, there was a great earthquake; and the sun became black as sackcloth of hair, and the moon became as blood: and the stars of heaven fell unto the earth, even as a fig tree casteth her untimely figs when she is shaken of a mighty wind. And the heaven departed as a scroll when it is rolled together; and every mountain and island were moved out of their places.

"And the kings of the earth, and the great men, and the rich men, and the chief captains, and the mighty men, and every bondman, and every free man, hid themselves in the dens and in the rocks of the mountains; and said to the mountains and rocks, Fall on us, and hide us from the face of him that sitteth on the throne, and from the wrath of the Lamb: for the great day of his wrath is come; and who shall be able to stand?"

"And after these things I saw four angels standing on the four corners of the earth, holding the four winds of the earth, that the wind should not blow on the earth, nor on the sea, nor on any tree. And I saw another angel ascending from the east, having the seal of the living God: and he cried with a loud voice to the four angels to whom it was given to hurt the earth and the sea, saying,

Angel: "Hurt not the earth, neither the sea, nor the trees, till we have sealed the servants of our God in their foreheads." . . .

John: "I beheld, and, lo, a great multitude which no man could number, of all nations and kindreds, and people, and tongues, stood before the throne, and before the Lamb, clothed with white robes, and palms in their hands; and cried with a loud voice, saying,

Redeemed Multitude: "Salvation to our God which sitteth upon the throne, and unto the Lamb.

John: "And all the angels stood round about the throne, and about the elders and the four beasts, and fell before the throne on their faces, and worshipped God, saying,

Angels: "Amen: Blessing, and glory, and wisdom, and thanksgiving, and honour, and power, and might, be unto our God for ever and ever. Amen."

John: "And one of the elders answered, saying unto me,

Elder: "What are these which are arrayed in white robes? and whence came they?"

John: "And I said unto him, Sir, thou knowest." . . .

Elder: "These are they which came out of great tribulation, and have washed their robes, and made them white in the blood of the Lamb. Therefore are they before the throne of God, and serve him day and night in his temple, and he that sitteth on the throne shall dwell among them. They shall hunger no more, neither thirst any more; neither shall the sun light on them, nor any heat. For the Lamb which is in the midst of the throne shall feed them, and shall lead them unto living fountains of waters: and God shall wipe away all tears from their eyes."

CHAPTER IV

The SEVEN SEALS—AGENCIES EMPLOYED

THE SECOND CYCLE, giving an account of the opening of the Seals, is not a new period in the history of the church. On the contrary, it presents again the Christian Dispensation from a different viewpoint. Like the others it covers the entire period from the incarnation of Christ to the end of the age. The new phase presented by the opening of the Seals is a revelation of the Agencies employed for fulfilling the purpose of God in the development of the Kingdom of God.

1—*The White Horse and Rider*

The opening of the first Seal is the signal for the first beast (living creature) to summon the rider upon the white horse by saying, "Come." Some have understood by this rider a world conqueror, or else the spirit of conquest, the horse being "white" because it is the beginning of his career and not yet blood-stained. The author of the "Four Horsemen of the Apocalypse" has popularized and given wide currency to this view. Some others interpret it as the symbol of counterfeit Christs, or the spirit of the "false Christs" predicted, in their effort to conquer the world.

The church, however, in all the ages has been practically unanimous in interpreting it as the conquering Christ entering upon His militant world career. Many have identified the rider on "the white horse" as the Gospel in its blessed mission of peaceful conquest, or else the church carrying the Gospel into all the world. This view differs but little from the ordinary interpretation which sees in the rider Christ Himself; and there seems to be no valid reason for personifying the Gospel as the rider upon the white horse. The difference between the two is so slight as to be immaterial.

It is consistent with the symbolism of the Apocalypse to recognize Christ as riding to His world conquest. It is a well recognized canon of interpretation, that there must be no confusion of terms, nor arbitrary use of symbols. The test of truth is its consistency with itself. The rider upon the white horse in the sixth chapter and in the nineteenth must be one and the same; and more especially would it be highly objectionable to allow the two to be symbolized by characters as antagonistic to each other as an ambitious world conqueror and the triumphant Christ. Compare Rev. 6:2 with Rev. 19:11-16, and the two representations fit perfectly as counterparts. In the first instance Christ starts on His campaign of conquest upon a white horse. In the other case the campaign is practically ended, and the conquering hero returns on a white horse attended by legions riding also upon white horses for the last Armageddon and the final victory. The church of the twentieth century is still singing,

> "The Son of God goes forth to war
> A Kingly crown to gain;"

and will so continue till the triumphant shout shall reverberate from heaven and be re-echoed on earth, "Alleluia for the Lord God omnipotent reigneth," as they "bring forth the royal diadem and crown Him Lord of all."

2—*The Symbol of War*

At the opening of the second Seal, and upon the call of the second beast (living creature) crying, "Come," "There went out another horse that was red, and power was given to him that sat thereon to take peace from the earth . . . and there was given unto him a great sword." There can be no mistaking of this rider and his mission. The rider on the white horse "was given a *crown;*" the rider on the red horse "was given a *sword.*" It is the symbol of War, red handed, stained in the blood of men in all the ages, the curse of humanity, the work of the devil, the fruit of sin, the devourer of property, the maker of widows and orphans and the cause of tears and sorrows unnumbered and of sufferings and agony unutterable—War, hideous monster, insatiable, drinking the life blood of the nations of earth.

Is War one of the Agencies employed for bringing in the Kingdom? Evil forces are not only over-ruled, but indirectly made to serve the righteous purposes of Him who "maketh the wrath of man to praise Him." Familiar cases abound in the old Testament where Israel by reason of wickedness and apostacy was subjected to war for purposes of discipline and to affect moral reformation. The Babylonian Captivity saved the nation from heathen conformity and was the final and desperate cure for idolatry.

The vision of the rider on the red horse is a warning that the same principle will prevail and the same extreme remedy be employed in the Christian Dispensation. Nations cannot appear as such, but only as individuals, at the great white throne and consequently are punished for national sins in the present life, war being one of the chief Agencies employed for the purpose. The World-War in some way, unknown as yet, perhaps saved Christian civilization. "What I do thou knowest not now."

It is God's prerogative not only to punish sin, but so to adjust human affairs as to correct the evil. In some way he will over-rule the deeds of wicked men—as in the case of Judah Iscariot—for the furtherance of the Kingdom. No bomb of Nihilist, no excess of Bolshevist, nor greedy grasp of ambitious Kaiser for world dominion, but is limited in its effect to some disciplinary purpose, which being accomplished, "the remainder of wrath will He restrain." In passing, attention is hereby directed briefly to the co-operation of human free-agency and divine sovereignty—the evil forces of the world actuated by their own ungodly ends in the unrestrained freedom of their own will yet blindly fulfilling the over-ruling purpose of divine providence for bringing in the Kingdom for the ultimate spiritual conquest of the world.

3—*Famine and Pestilence*

The rider on the black horse—Famine—and the rider on the pale horse—Pestilence—may well be considered together. They are the natural consequences of war and usually follow in its wake. Famines and pestilences are regarded in the light of "dispensations of providence." The consequences of human folly are often laid at the door of providence. Frequently they are partly due to human faults and partly due to natural causes, but are in either event in the hand of the Lord of heaven and earth. "The King's heart is in the hand of the Lord, he turneth it whithersoever he will"—and so are the forces of nature. "The stars in their courses fought against Sisera."

The Plagues of Egypt were due partly to natural causes, but were so timed of God as to overthrow Pharaoh and the Egyptians, enemies of God's people. Famine and pestilence fall into the same category as war, used of God to punish wickedness and to discipline His church, indirectly advancing the Kingdom. "All these things are against me," wailed Jacob in his mistaken blindness. "All things work together for good" argued Paul, having a clearer conception of divine providence.

As revealing the extent of the ravages wrought by the destructive Agencies of the past decade alone, the New York Times says that war, pestilence, famine, and cataclysms of nature have taken toll of 62,000,000 human lives since the outbreak of the World-War. This is the estimate advanced at Washington by the assistant director of the league of Red Cross societies. By categories war has accounted for 9,000,000 lives, civil war for 6,000,000, famine for 6,000,000, epidemic for 40,000,000, and earthquake and flood for 2,000,000. The Times says: "First in rank among the visitations of nature has been the influenza, the secret of which is still to be traced and mastered. It has been estimated that between May, 1918, and March, 1919, the 'flu' took 25,000,000 lives, or not far from 2 per cent of the entire population of the world. In India it has been deduced from the results of the census of 1921 that between twelve and thirteen million people must have perished during the epidemic. Entire regions of Africa were swept clean of life, and one can only conjecture what the death totals were in the interior of the continent, concerning which no definite information is available. In the United States the deaths in 1918-'19 were nearly 550,000, and the total for the five years up to 1923 has been estimated at 750,000. The outbreak of 1922, though less virulent, took nearly 17,000 lives in Great Britain during the first three months of the year . . . Soviet Russia has felt the scourge of war, of civil war, of famine and of pestilence. The first and the last she shared with the rest of the world. Civil war and famine have been almost peculiarly her own. There is little doubt that the 6,000,000 deaths credited to civil strife are nearly all to be allocated to the Bolshevist revolution and the civil wars that followed. Similarly the 6,000,000 lives taken by famine would be almost entirely Russian lives, with a small allowance for China . . . Between 1914 and 1924 there disappeared from the soil of what is now the Soviet republic something like 20,000,000 people. . . . The present Soviet Russia had in 1914 a population of about 150,000,000, or roughly 10 per cent of the world's population. But this 10 per cent of population contributed during the next decade from 25 per cent to 35 per cent of the casualties for the entire world."

4—*Intercession of Saints*

In the opening of the fifth Seal the scene shifts from earth to heaven. "I saw under the altar the souls of them that were slain for the Word of God and for the testimony which they held. And they cried with a loud voice, saying, 'How long, O Lord' . . . and white robes were from them;" and they were urged to patience.

> "His purposes will ripen fast unfolding every hour,
> The bud may have a bitter taste, but sweet will be the flower."

Intercession as a means of bringing in the Kingdom is not confined to earth. "The saints in heaven and on earth but one communion make" and have common aspirations and interests. The prayers of the redeemed in glory and of suffering saints on earth are partial means to the fulfilment of the divine purpose. "More things are wrought by prayer than this world dreams of."

The blood of the martyrs in all ages "from the blood of righteous Abel unto the blood of Zacherias, son of Barachias," is in itself an impersonal appeal to the divine attribute of Justice for vindication and for the intervention of "the Judge of all the earth" in behalf of his suffering church. The appeal of the martyrs is based upon faith in the ultimate triumph of righteousness:

"Right is right as God is God,
And right the day must win.
To doubt would be disloyalty,
To falter would be sin."

Huss, condemned to join "the noble army of martyrs," appealed from the human tribunal to the heavenly, and summoned his judges to meet him and answer at the bar of divine justice. Latimer at the stake encouraged his companion in tribulation saying: "Master Ridley we will kindle such a fire this day as shall never be extinguished."

"Speak, History! who are Life's victors?
Unroll thy long annals and say,
Are they those whom the world called the victors—
Who won the success of a day?
The martyrs, or Nero? The Spartans who
Fell at Thermopylae's tryst
Or the Persians and Xerxes? His judges
Or Socrates? Pilate or Christ?"

Whether these "souls of them that were slain for the Word of God, and for the testimony which they held," were limited to the martyrs of the first century, or whether they were the vast multitudes which have suffered during the entire militant age of Christianity, is immaterial. The faith of God's noblest saints is often severely tested by the long delay in answer to their prayers—involving implicit trust in the righteousness and faithfulness of "the Judge of all the earth." Inquiry even in heaven raises the same question of this incomprehensible delay, as the martyrs "cried with a loud voice, saying, How long, O Lord, will thou not judge and avenge our blood on them that dwell on the earth." To which questioning, was given substantially the identical reply as that vouchsafed to suffering saints on earth by Christ. "Shall not God avenge his own elect, which cry day and night unto him, though he bear long with them" inquires Jesus, who answers His own query with the emphatic assurance, "I tell you that he will avenge them speedily."

5—*The End of the Dispensation*

The opening of the sixth Seal reveals once again the end of the Dispensation.

"And I beheld when he had opened the sixth seal, and, lo, there was a great earthquake; and the sun became black as sackcloth of hair, and the moon became as blood; and the stars of heaven fell unto the earth, even as a fig tree casteth her untimely figs, when she is shaken of a mighty wind. And the heaven departed as a scroll when it is rolled together; and every mountain and island were moved out of their places.

"And the kings of the earth, and the great men, and the rich men, and the chief captains, and the mighty men, and every bondman, and every free man, hid themselves in the dens and in the rocks of the mountains; and said to the mountains and rocks, Fall on us, and hide us from the face of him that sitteth on the throne, and from the wrath of the lamb: for the great day of his wrath is come; and who shall be able to stand?"

The first Cycle ended, as narrated in the previous chapter, with the Second Coming. The second contains an additional feature, the Judgment Scene—"the great day of wrath." Some see in this language only the fall of Jerusalem; others, the destruction of the Turkish Empire, or similar upheaval and downfall of nations. Possibly it may have indirect reference to the catastrophe with which the Jewish Dispensation ended; but if so, only as a type and symbol of the universal cataclysm at the close of the present age. This language of the Apocalypse is practically identical with the terms used by Christ in describing the end of the age: "The sun shall be darkened and the moon shall not give his light and the stars shall fall from heaven and the powers of the heaven shall be shaken. And then shall appear the sign of the Son of man in heaven: and then shall all the tribes of the earth mourn, and they shall see the Son of man coming in the clouds of heaven with power and great glory."—Matt. 24:29, 30.

6—*The Interlude*

Now comes the Interlude in the seventh chapter with its chorus of consolation. The earthly scene of the Drama is dark with war, famine and pestilence, ending in catastrophe amid earthquake and other convulsions of nature with men calling to rocks and mountains to hide them from the wrath of the Lamb. The Interlude introduces the heavenly scene: "The four angels . . . holding the four winds of earth" are forbidden to loose these agencies of destruction till the servants of God are sealed and rendered immune to the disasters afflicting earth's inhabitants—"one hundred and forty and four thousand" being the number of the sealed.

This is followed by the Chorus of the Redeemed. "A great multitude, which no man could number, of all nations and kindreds and people and tongues stood before the throne and before the Lamb, clothed with white robes and palms in their hands; and cried with a loud voice, saying: "Salvation to our God which sitteth upon the throne, and unto the Lamb." Then in antiphony comes the mighty response of "all the angels round about the throne saying,

> "Amen—Blessing and glory and wisdom
> And thanksgiving and honour and power and might
> Be unto our God forever and ever.—Amen."

This Chorus of Consolation is then strikingly supplemented by the colloquy between heaven and earth:

One of the Elders: "What are these which are arrayed in white robes and whence came they?"

John: "Sir, thou knowest."

Elder: "These are they which came out of great tribulation, and have washed their robes, and made them white in the blood of the Lamb. Therefore are they before the throne of God, and serve him day and night in his temple: and he that sitteth on the throne shall dwell among them.

"They shall hunger no more, neither thirst any more; neither shall the sun light on them, nor any heat. For the Lamb which is in the midst of the throne shall feed them, and shall lead them unto living fountains of waters: and God shall wipe away all tears from their eyes."

The significance of the Interlude with its chorus is too manifest for extended comment: On earth woes—"unmerciful disaster follows fast and follows faster"—men overwhelmed with unutterable agony in the great day of wrath, yet God's people untouched, unmoved, undisturbed, sealed against disaster, shouting their peans of glory and waving their palm branches of victory. From the divine standpoint, they are numbered, "one hundred and forty and four thousand"—not intended as exhaustive but symbolical of completeness. From the human standpoint, however, they constitute "a great multitude which no man could number."

Possibly the "one hundred and forty and four thousand" may symbolize Jewish saints, while the numberless multitude represents those from among Gentile nations. It matters not. The Consolation is the same. The redeemed—in the divine comprehension—are known, numbered, preserved. In the inadequate mathematics of earth, they are innumerable, glorified—the ransomed of the Lord filling the city of the New Jerusalem with hallelujahs of praise, "unto him that sitteth on the throne and unto the Lamb forever and ever. Amen."

The THIRD CYCLE

TEXT: CHAPTERS VIII-XI

John: "And when he had opened the seventh seal, there was silence in heaven about the space of half an hour. And I saw the seven angels which stood before God; and to them were given seven trumpets.

"And another angel came and stood at the altar, having a golden censer; and there was given unto him much incense, that he should offer it with the prayers of all saints upon the golden altar which was before the throne. And the smoke of the incense, which came with the prayers of the saints, ascended up before God out of the angel's band.

"And the angel took the censer, and filled it with fire of the altar, and cast it into the earth: and there were voices, and thunderings, and lightnings, and an earthquake. And the seven angels which had the seven trumpets prepared themselves to sound. And I beheld, and heard an angel flying through the midst of heaven, saying with a loud voice,

Angel: "Woe, woe, woe, to the inhabiters of the earth by reason of the other voices of the trumpet of the three angels, which are yet to sound!"

John: "And the fifth angel sounded, and I saw a star fall from heaven unto the earth: and to him was given the key of the bottomless pit. One woe is past; and, behold, there come two woes more hereafter. And the sixth angel sounded, and I heard a voice from the four horns of the golden altar which is before God, saying to the sixth angel which had the trumpet,

Angel: "Loose the four angels which are bound in the great river Euphrates."

John: "And the angel which I saw stand upon the sea and upon the earth lifted up his hand to heaven, and sware by him that liveth for ever and ever, who created heaven, and the things that therein are, and the earth, and the things that therein are, and the sea, and the things which are therein, that there should be time no longer: but in the days of the voice of the seventh angel, when he shall begin to sound, the mystery of God should be finished, as he hath declared to his servants the prophets.

"And the seventh angel sounded; and there were great voices in heaven, saying, The kingdoms of this world are become the kingdoms of our Lord, and of his Christ; and he shall reign for ever and ever. And the four and twenty elders, which sat before God on their seats, fell upon their faces, and worshipped God, saying,

Elders: "We give thee thanks, O Lord God Almighty, which art, and wast, and art to come; because thou hast taken to thee thy great power and has reigned. And the nations were angry, and thy wrath is come, and the time of the dead, that they should be judged, and that thou shouldest give reward unto thy servants the prophets, and to the saints, and they that fear thy name, small and great; and shouldest destroy them which destroy the earth.

"And the temple of God was opened in heaven, and there was seen in his temple the ark of his testament: and there were lightnings, and voices, and thunderings, and an earthquake, and great hail."

CHAPTER V

The SEVEN TRUMPETS JUDGMENTS UPON *the* WORLD

THE THIRD CYCLE, covering Chapters VIII to XI inclusive, reveals the realms affected by the Judgments of God upon an ungodly world, ushered in by the sounding of the Seven Trumpets. The panorama begins by exhibiting first an angel with a golden censer offering incense, mingled with the prayers of the saints, which ascended in a cloud of smoke before the throne. The response was the same censer filled with fire from off the altar cast into the earth, causing "voices and thunderings and lightnings and an earthquake."

Is there not thereby revealed the intimate relation between heaven and earth, as well as the spiritual power of prayer as one of the tremendous influences affecting the entire universe? The intercessions in heaven, whether originating among the redeemed in glory or ascending from the church on earth, find an echo in the affairs of men resulting in judgments upon the ungodly. It is practically the same incident revealing the same purpose as the cry of the martyrs for vindication in the previous panorama, saying, "How long, O Lord," starting waves in eternity which beat upon the shores of time. Dean Alford accordingly intimates that "the judgments which follow are answers to these prayers of the saints and are inflicted on the enemies of the church"—justified evidently by the context.

Synchronous But not Repetitions

Always it must be borne in mind that each Cycle is synchronous with all the others but not mere repetitions. Each is an entirely new panorama which adds new features as well as repeating some common to the others—exhibitions of the same principles under different aspects and in different circumstances, but in an ascending climax of Judgments.

This may be strikingly re-enforced, illustrated and more vividly presented by a suggestive comparison prepared for the purpose by Professor Milligan:

SEALS		TRUMPETS			VIALS		
Chap. vi		Chap. viii			Chap. xvi		
1.	Earth	1.	Earth	Land	1.	Earth	Land
2.		2.		Sea	2.		Sea
3.		3.		Rivers, etc.	3		Rivers, etc
4.		4		Sun, etc.	4		Sun,

Observe that the Trumpets and Vials next coincide in a most remarkable feature which was omitted in the Seals:

SIXTH NUMBER

TRUMPETS	VIALS
Chap. ix. 13	Chap. xvi. 12
The river Euphrates	The river Euphrates

The identity of the three Cycles is still further manifest in their conclusion:

SEVENTH NUMBER

SEALS	TRUMPETS	VIALS
Chap. vi. 12-14	Chap. xi. 15	Chap. xvi. 17
The close of all.	The close of all.	The close of all.

While these Cycles coincide as to the period of time covered, each in the narrative follows the others from the necessity of the case. John could not possibly have seen all these visions at one and the same time; and it would have been equally impossible for the reader to apprehend their various features except by their presentation in separate panoramas. They parallel each other but in no sense are they mere repetitions. They present the same underlying principles of the Christian Dispensation with marked variations of circumstance and detail. The Seals are more general in character; but while the Trumpets and Vials are more striking in their similarity and details, the Trumpets herald the judgments of God upon an ungodly world, and the Vials represent the outpouring of divine wrath chiefly upon an apostate Church.

Symbols of Judgment

Trumpets are not simply heralds of coming events, but are more distinctively alarms summoning the hosts of an army to battle, and are often intimately associated with the judgments of God: "Blow ye the trumpet in Zion and sound the alarm in my holy mountain; let all the inhabitants of the earth tremble: for the day of the Lord cometh, and it is nigh at hand."—Joel 2:1.

The Judgments of God fall with peculiar force upon the world but to a certain extent affect the peace and serenity of the saints as well. The church is in the midst of the world, intimately associated with its welfare, engaged in the same occupations, discharging the same duties, exposed to the same trials and mingling in the same peaceful arts. Some of the plagues of Egypt affect Israel as well but not to the same extent. The difference begins to emerge in the immunity of Israel from the later plagues, reaching the climax in the salvation of Israel and the utter destruction of Egypt. The saints share, to a certain extent, the fortunes and misfortunes of their fellow men in wars, pestilences and other temporal judgments, but are unscathingly preserved, being "sealed" against the extreme penalty, thereby escaping the fearful destruction of the ungodly element of society.—Rev. 9:4.

Distinctive Features

Examining several special features of the vision of the Trumpets, one of the most conspicuous is the evident fact that the symbolism is taken largely from the plagues of Egypt—"hail," water turned into "blood," "locusts," etc. The other significant fact is that these plagues fell in full force solely upon Egypt, the oppressor of God's Israel, typifying judgments upon an ungodly world, the enemy of spiritual Israel.

The first three Trumpets affect "the earth," "the sea" and "the rivers," while the fourth shifts to the heavenly bodies, sun, moon and stars, resulting in the destruction of a third part of each. Why exactly "a third" finds its explanation, perhaps, in the symbolism attached to numbers upon which the Apocalypse is based and about which interpreters often disagree.

The sounding of the fifth Trumpet reveals a star fallen from heaven unto the earth; "and to him was given the key of the bottomless pit," which being opened emits "smoke as of a great furnace," the sun and the air being darkened, producing locusts as scorpions. This probably corresponds to the casting out of Satan from heaven, narrated in Chapter 12:9 of the next vision and mentioned also by Christ who notified His disciples at the time saying: "I beheld Satan as lightning fall from heaven."—Luke 10:18. The similarity of the language used in describing each case is too striking to admit of strong reasonable doubt.

These scourging locusts, unearthly monsters, shaped like horses, belligerent in strength, with teeth like lions cruel and devouring, with breastplates of iron protecting them from attack in their marauding onslaughts and with stings in their tails as scorpions—under the direction and control of "a king over them which is the angel of the bottomless pit, whose name in the Hebrew tongue is Abaddon but in the Greek tongue hath his name Apolyon"—constitute a terrifying symbolism describing the demons and evil forces appointed to afflict the ungodly in executing the judgments of God. Unquestionably it is figurative language; but figures of speech are employed to characterize things which cannot be expressed in ordinary terms of speech.

Referring to this dreadful eruption from the empire of darkness, the announcement portends anything but comfort for an ungodly world: "One woe is past; and behold, there come two more woes hereafter." Interpreters of the "historic" order explain this first "woe" as Mohammed or some similar curse of mankind, with, however, no agreement among themselves, a sufficient refutation of the futility of a guessing contest.

The sixth Trumpet is the signal for loosing "the four angels which were bound in the great river Euphrates," issuing in the marshalling of a vast army of horsemen—"two hundred thousand thousand" . . . Having breastplates of fire, and jacinth and brimstone: and the heads of the horses were as the heads of lions; and out of their mouths issued fire and smoke and brimstone." This fearful scourge of ungodliness results in the destruction of "the third part of men." The significance of the reference to the "Euphrates" is doubtless due to the historic fact that from this region came incessantly the hordes of Assyrians, inveterate and cruel enemies of ancient Israel, executing judgments upon the wicked monarchy, eventuating in the carrying away into captivity both the Kingdoms of Israel and Judah. If the "locusts" of "the first woe" suggests judgments upon Egyptian oppression, possibly the Euphrates-scourge of "the second woe" alludes to the events connected with the Babylonish Captivity, both being faint types of the modern forces of evil which will execute the judgments of God on an ungodly world.

Impenitence, the Climax of Sin

The most significant statement, however, is that "the rest of the men which were not killed by these plagues yet repented not of the works of their hands"—enumerating a long and dark catalogue of evil deeds. The sufferings of God's people are disciplinary; but the judgments upon the world are punitive, having no remedial intent and effect. Instead of penitence, the wicked in all ages blaspheme God as the source of their sufferings. Christ's severest denunciations of sin fell upon "the cities wherein most of his mighty works were done," not because of the number and heinousness of their sin, but "because they repented not.'"—Matt.

11:20. This is a sufficient demonstration of the mercy of God who "doth not willingly afflict," and who "hath no pleasure in the death of the wicked," but whose judgments fall upon the incorrigible. Impenitence likewise is a vindication of the Justice of God and a sufficient explanation of the existence and necessity of hell itself—the awful blot in the universe of God. Its inmates are doomed not because they were "sinners above all men," whose guilt transcended the mercy of God. Pointing to the woes of "the bottomless pit" exemplified in the agony of lost souls, an angel from heaven can give no other explanation of their fate than that "they repented not." No wonder the merciful Christ, "the Lamb for sinners slain," sounds the fearful warning: "Except ye repent ye shall all likewise perish." Is there any other possible alternative?

The Two Witnesses

The purpose of this study does not call for an examination and explanation of the full details of each item and incident of the various sections of the Apocalyptic vision; yet a passing comment is due perhaps the "two witnesses," introduced in this Cycle just before the Seventh Trumpet sounds the doom of the ungodly world with which the Dispensation ends. Interpreters of the "Historic" regime identify them with Luther and the Reformation. Dean Alford suggests Moses and Elijah. Others regard them as representatives of the Old and New Testament Dispensations.

More in keeping with the purpose of the Apocalypse is the suggestion that they symbolize the spirit of the martyrs of all the ages—"martyr" being the Greek word for "witness." In the first Cycle they are "cast into prison" by Satan and "have tribulation ten days" and are promised "a crown of life." In the Second, they are represented as having "come out of great tribulation and have washed their robes and made them white in the blood of the Lamb . . . and are before the throne of God and serve him day and night in his temple." In this third Cycle after they "have finished their testimony, the beast that ascendeth out of the bottomless pit shall make war against them, and shall overcome them and kill them . . . And they heard a great voice from heaven saying unto them, "Come up hither. And they ascended up to heaven in a cloud." In the last Cycle, Rev. 20:4, John saw them again as "the souls of them that were beheaded for the witness of Jesus and for the word of God. . . . And they lived and reigned with Christ a thousand years." Testimony, martyrdom and crowns are featured in these various visions, reminding the saints that they "must through much tribulation enter into the Kingdom of God."

The Spirit of Martyrdom

The message that pervades the entire Apocalypse, running through all of its visions, is that the spirit of martyrdom is the common lot of God's people. Not all of them are called upon to seal their testimony with their blood and join the select number designated "the noble army of martyrs," but all must "follow his steps" by the way of the cross. Christ himself submitted to the inevitable law, "Except a corn of wheat fall into the earth and die, it abideth alone, but if it die, it bringeth forth much fruit."

"Who follows in his train?" Not simply "that martyr first whose eagle eye could pierce beyond the grave," but the entire body of believers—everyone of whom "overcometh"—a vast multitude whose martyrdom constitutes the chief lesson of the Apocalypse. It knows no Christianity that does not in one way or another conduct the believer through tears and blood, through fire and flame, through suffering and the cross to the heavenly reward, bestowed by the hand of the Master himself in the crowning day, celebrating the triumph of Christ and His victorious blood-stained hosts.

The End of the Dispensation

The sounding of the Seventh Trumpet brings us again to the end of the Dispensation amid the convulsions of nature as in the case of the former Cycles, but adds two additional features:

1. There were great voices in heaven, saying, "The kingdoms of this world are become the kingdoms of our Lord and of his Christ: and he shall reign forever and ever." 2. "Thy wrath is come and the *time of the dead, that they should be judged,* and that thou shouldest give reward unto thy servants the prophets and to the saints."

At the close of each Cycle the end of the Dispensation is described, each time in clearer fuller terms till now universal dominion is proclaimed for Christ, and the judgment of *"the dead,"* in connection with the reward of the righteous. If any doubt remained that each account brings us to the end of the age, that uncertainty would surely and forever be swept away by the plain statement here of the judgment of the dead. It has been contended by some that the judgment of the righteous and their awards would precede "the judgment of the great white throne:" but the two events are joined together here in the same irresistible statement. No amount of argument can impeach the fact they are announced as simultaneous, or at least following in quick succession.

The Interlude

In former Cycles the Interlude with its Chorus followed the description of the end of the age, but in this case they coincide. The mighty angel standing with one foot upon the land and the other upon the sea had sworn "by him that liveth forever and ever," "that there should be time no longer"—more correctly rendered that there would be "no further delay." "But in the days of the voice of the seventh angel, when he shall begin to sound, the mystery of God should be finished."

Now the Seventh Trumpet having sounded the doom of the world, at that exact moment the heavenly Chorus sings its consolation amid the very convulsions with which the Dispensation ends: "There were great voices in heaven saying:

"The kingdoms of this world are become
The kingdoms of our Lord and of his Christ,
And he shall reign forever and ever."

"And the four and twenty elders, which sat before God on their seats, fell upon their faces and worshipped God, saying:

"We give thee thanks O Lord God Almighty
Which art and wast and art to come,
Because thou hast taken to thee
Thy great name and hast reigned,
And the nations were angry,
And thy wrath is come,
And the time of the dead
That they should be judged;
And that thou shouldest give reward
Unto thy servants, the prophets and to the saints,
And to them that fear thy name.
And should destroy them that destroy the earth."

As in the other Cycles, so in this, the earth being cursed with ungodliness is convulsed with cataclysms under the righteous judgments of God; but heaven sings consolation in the triumph of righteousness and of the conquering Christ, giving full assurance of the blessed awards of the saints as sharing the glory of their Lord unto the ages of the ages.

The FOURTH CYCLE

TEXT: CHAPTERS XII-XIV

John: "And there appeared a great wonder in heaven; a woman clothed with the sun, and the moon under her feet, and upon her head a crown of twelve stars: and she being with child cried, travailing in birth, and pained to be delivered. And there appeared another wonder in heaven; and behold a great red dragon, having seven heads and ten horns, and seven crowns upon his heads. And his tail drew the third part of the stars of heaven, and did cast them to the earth, and the dragon stood before the woman which was ready to be delivered, for to devour her child as soon as it was born.

"And she brought forth a man child, who was to rule all nations with a rod of iron: and her child was caught up unto God, and to his throne. And the woman fled into the wilderness, where she hath a place prepared of God, that they should feed her there a thousand two hundred and threescore days.

"And there was war in heaven: Michael and his angels fought against the dragon; and the dragon fought and his angels, and prevailed not; neither was their place found any more in heaven. And the great dragon was cast out, that old serpent, called the Devil, and Satan, which deceiveth the whole world: he was cast out into the earth, and his angels were cast out with him. And I heard a loud voice saying in heaven,

Voice in Heaven: "Now is come salvation, and strength, and the kingdom of our God, and the power of his Christ: for the accuser of our brethren is cast down, which accused them before our God day and night. And they overcame him by the blood of the Lamb, and by the word of their testimony; and they loved not their lives unto the death.

"Therefore rejoice, ye heavens, and ye that dwell in them. Woe to the inhabiters of the earth and of the sea! for the devil is come down unto you, having great wrath, because he knoweth that he hath but a short time." . . .

John: "And I stood upon the sand of the sea, and saw a beast rise up out of the sea, having seven heads and ten horns, and upon his horns ten crowns, and upon his heads the name of blasphemy. And the beast which I saw was like unto a leopard, and his feet were as the feet of a bear, and his mouth as the mouth of a lion: and the dragon gave him his power, and his seat, and great authority. And I saw one of his heads as it were wounded to death; and his deadly wound was healed: and all the world wondered after the beast. . . .

"And I beheld another beast coming up out of the earth; and he had two horns like a Lamb, and he spake as a dragon. And he exerciseth all the power of the first beast before him, and causeth the earth and them which dwell therein to worship the first beast, whose deadly wound was healed. And he doeth great wonders, so that he maketh fire come down from heaven on the earth in the sight of men. . . .

"And that no man might buy or sell, save he that had the mark, or the name of the beast, or the number of his name. Here is wisdom. Let him that hath understanding count the number of the beast: for it is the number of a man; and his number is six hundred thereescore and six.

"And I looked, and lo, a Lamb stood on the mount Sion, and with him an hundred forty and four thousand, having his Father's name written in their foreheads.

"And I heard a voice from heaven, as the voice of many waters, and as the voice of a great thunder: and I heard the voice of harpers harping with their harps: and they sung as it were a new song before the throne, and before the four beasts, and the elders: and no man could learn that song but the hundred and forty and four thousand, which were redeemed from the earth. . . .

"And I saw another angel fly in the midst of heaven, having the everlasting gospel to preach unto them that dwell on the earth, and to every nation and kindred, and tongue, and people; saying with a loud voice,

First Angel: "Fear God, and give glory to him; for the hour of his judgment is come, and worship him that made heaven, and earth, and the sea, and the fountains of waters."

Second Angel: "And there followed another angel, saying, Babylon is fallen, is fallen, that great city, because she made all nations drink of the wine of the wrath of her fornication."

Third Angel: "And the third angel followed them, saying with a loud voice, If any man worship the beast and his image, and receive his mark in his forehead, or in his hand, the same shall drink of the wine of the wrath of God, which is poured out without mixture into the cup of his indignation; and he shall be tormented with fire and brimstone in the presence of the holy angels, and in the presence of the Lamb." . . .

John: "And I heard a voice from heaven saying unto me:

Voice in Heaven: "Write, Blessed are the dead which die in the Lord from henceforth: Yea, saith the Spirit, that they may rest from their labours; and their works do follow them."

John: "And I looked, and behold a white cloud, and upon the cloud one sat like unto the Son of man, having on his head a golden crown, and in his hand a sharp sickle. And another angel came out of the temple, crying with a loud voice to him that sat on the cloud:

Angel: "Thrust in thy sickle, and reap: for the time is come for thee to reap; for the harvest of the earth is ripe."

John: "And he that sat on the cloud thrust in his sickle on the earth; and the earth was reaped. And another angel came out from the altar, which had power over fire: and cried with a loud cry to him that had the sharp sickle, saying:

Angel: "Thrust in thy sharp sickle, and gather the clusters of the vine of the earth: for her grapes are fully ripe."

John: "And the angel thrust in his sickle into the earth, and gathered the vine of the earth, and cast it into the great winepress of the wrath of God."

CHAPTER VI

The DRAGON *and* TWO BEASTS TRINITY *of* EVIL

THE last Cycle ends with the judgment of the dead, and the fourth opens with the birth of Christ. Could there be clearer refutation of the continuous "historic" interpretation of the Apocalypse? How can there be any other rational explanation of the fact, that here the Incarnation of Christ is introduced after the judgment of the dead than the interpretation herein advocated: That the Apocalypse presents the Christian Dispensation again and again from different viewpoints? Its supreme purpose is to present great spiritual principles characteristic of the Dispensation rather than the prediction of future events.

The Trinity of Hell

Carrying out the symbolism of numbers, some have designated this Cycle as the vision of the Seven Mystic Persons: The Woman, her Son, her Seed, the Archangel Michael, the Dragon, the Beast from the Sea and the Beast from the land. Even if this suggestion has any merit, it would still remain true that the special purpose of this vision is to exhibit the three great enemies of the church, the dragon and the two beasts.

As there is a Trinity of Heaven, the Father, the Son and the Holy Ghost; so there is revealed in this Cycle a Trinity of evil, the dragon and the beasts. Just as Christ Himself encountered three enemies, the Roman Empire, the Jewish Apostacy and Satan, so the church and each individual Christian must contend with the same corresponding three, "the world, the flesh and the devil." They are the same in all the ages. Satan the chief, symbolized as "the dragon, that old serpent," is called "the devil"—the common enemy of God and man. The first beast symbolizes the Roman Empire, the spirit of "the world." The second beast, elsewhere called "the false prophet," corresponds to "the flesh," the evil within the church itself.

The Two Marvels in Heaven

The "great wonder in heaven," the "woman clothed with the sun . . . travailing in birth," is unquestionably the church —whether Jewish or Christian matters little. God has only one church, though existing under different Dispensations, or called by various denominational names.

The second "wonder in heaven," "the great red dragon," is later identified as "that old serpent called the devil and Satan." His effort to "devour the child as soon as it was born" in a historic fact. The first attempt was made through the agency of Herod who slew the children of Bethlehem; his second, the temptation of the wilderness; and his last, by means of the cross—blindly bringing to pass the purpose of God for the redemption of His people.

Divine Intervention

The flight of the woman "into the wilderness, where she hath a place prepared of God, that they should feed her there a thousand, two hundred and threescore days," mentioned again in the same chapter as covering a period of "a time, and times and a half time," is the same event revealing the divine intervention and preservation of the saints—alike the seed of the woman and of her Son. The account is repeated not because they deal with two separate events, nor for the sake of double assurance. The first refers to the divine purpose, the eternal decree guaranteeing the safety of the elect. The second describes the actual fact, the fulfilment of the divine promise, standing in the relation to each other of cause and effect.

"Time and Times and a Half Time"

In the previous Cycle, Jerusalem is to be "trodden under foot of the Gentiles," "forty and two months"—twelve hundred and sixty days. The two witnesses were to "prophesy a thousand two hundred and threescore days." Elsewhere this same period is spoken of as "three years and a half." Whether counted in years, months or days, the time-equivalent is the same. It is borrowed from the prophecy of Daniel, the Old Testament Apocalypse —Daniel 7:25, 12:7.

It has been variously interpreted. In length of time it corresponds to the earthly ministry of Christ, to the period of persecution under Nero and to duration of the Jewish War. Does it have a literal application; or does it follow the usual law of numbers in this symbolic book? Many interpret it as a symbolic equivalent for twelve hundred and sixty years—a day for a year. By calculations dating its beginning from some special event, men in all ages have announced "the time is just about to expire." Despite these calculations, "historic" fulfilments and observances of "the signs of the times," the significance of this symbolic number has not yet been made known. It still remains true of all prophetic forecastings as was announced by Christ Himself: "But of that day and that hour knoweth no man, no, not the angels which are in heaven, neither the son but the Father."—Mark 13:32. "It is not for you to know the times or the seasons which the Father hath put in his own power."—Acts 1:7.

Milligan understands this number to symbolize the whole period of the Christian Dispensation. Others insist that as the number seven stands for perfection, so the "three and a half"—one-half of seven—means simply indefiniteness. All of these vagaries are additional proofs that the Apocalypse is not a book of predictions but of principles. Any attempt at calculations, or identifying historic events by means of its figures or symbols, will inevitably lead to the wildest of fancies and away from the spiritual purport of its real meaning.

"War in Heaven"

"And there was war in heaven: Michael and his angels fought against the dragon and the dragon fought and his angels. And prevailed not; neither was their place found any more in heaven." This raises the question as to the mysterious origin of evil and the time of the war in heaven—neither of which is revealed in Scripture. Poetry and theological speculation have played their part in the effort to be "wise above that which is written"—in vain.

Milton in Paradise Lost gives the most graphic account in his avowed purpose "to assert eternal providence and justify the ways of God to men." The fall of Satan is supposed to antedate the creation of man; and his scheme to destroy God's workmanship and his attack on Adam and Eve in Eden are prompted by jealousy and bitter hatred of God and all his works. Instead of being thwarted by Satan, it provokes the most marvelous love of God, and Satan himself is thwarted in Paradise Regained.

Pember's Theory—Specimen

In "Earth's Earliest Ages," George H. Pember, of England, fifty years ago, promulgated an original and striking theory, endorsed by the late Dr. A. J. Gordon, of Boston, as a most plausible explanation of Satan's office, fall and present evil purposes. His book is as readable as a romance, and his theory is as worthy of consideration as any human speculative explanation of the world's prehistoric ages.

According to Pember's conception, based upon obscure Scriptural hints, Satan was one of the highest of all God's creation (see Ezekiel 28:13-15) placed in charge of this world of spirits as "overlord" (Psalm 82); being still spoken of as "the Prince of this world."—John 14:32. Lifted up with pride he attempted independent lordship, and in his rebellion carried his earthly subjects into antagonism to God, the Creator and Supreme Ruler of the universe. This introduction of evil into the world accounts for the cataclysms that occurred before the creation of man, rendering it "empty and void," which required recreation at the hands of God, described at the beginning of Genesis.

The creation of the human race to take the place of Satan and his subjects was bitterly resented, and Satan marshalled all his forces and summoned all his ingenuity to destroy the workmanship of God and drag the human race down with him in his fall. This accounts for the temptation and fall in Eden. Pember sees in the mixed marriages of the Antediluvians, which filled the earth with violence, evidence of Satanic scheming. As yet Satan had not been expelled from his office as overlord of earth, and his demons had power to incarnate themselves and form marriages with the daughters of men, which necessitated the flood to destroy these superhuman monsters.

Pember further bases his theory of Satan's overlordship on such Scriptures as Job 1:7 where he, among other officials, presents himself before God, as yet, not "cast out" but as the "accuser" of Job and other saints.—Rev. 12:9-10. Satan was finally deprived of his lordship over earth, being conquered and bound by Christ, Who supplants him as Lord of earth. Demoniacal possession is explained as showing Satan still possessed a power over men which Christ destroyed by "casting out devils."

According to this theory, Satan in the closing days of the present Dispensation will again be "loosed," recover part of his power for the final assault in Armageddon. Pember sees in the "unclean spirits like frogs" which came "out of the mouth of the dragon and out of the mouth of the beast and out of the mouth of the false prophet," described in the next Cycle — Rev. 16:13 — a revival of demoniacal possession now manifesting itself in modern Spiritualism, "materializations" and kindred phenomena—quoting as proof: "For they are the spirits of devils, working miracles, which go forth unto the Kings of the earth, and of the whole world, to gather them to the battle of that great day of God Almighty."

Milton and Pember are quoted here to direct attention to the fact that the fall of Satan and his "casting out" of heaven did not take place at the same time. His fall evidently preceded, and accounts for, that of Adam. In this twelfth chapter of Revelation the war in heaven and the casting out of Satan are introduced in connection with the Incarnation of Christ, which seems to indicate that event as the date. It is probably the same event which is described later as the "binding" of Satan—deprived of his power. Christ Himself refers to the same, saying, "I saw Satan as lightning fall from heaven."

The event is joyfully celebrated in heaven: "And I heard a great voice saying in heaven:

> "Now is come salvation and strength,
> And the kingdom of our God,
> And the power of his Christ;
> For the accuser of our brethren is cast down,
> Which accused them day and night before our God.
> And they overcame him by the blood of the Lamb,
> And by the word of their testimony:
> And they loved not their lives unto the death.
> Therefore, rejoice ye heaven
> And ye that dwell in them."

The First Beast

The second enemy of the church is the beast from the sea, "having seven heads and ten horns . . . like unto a leopard . . . the feet of a bear . . . the mouth of a lion; and the dragon gave him his seat and great authority . . . and power was given unto him to continue forty and two months"—the same mystic number. He incorporates all the features of the four beasts of Daniel 7, which may possibly be the Key to the interpretation. In Daniel each beast represents a world-kingdom power—the most terrible symbolizing the Roman Empire.

This beast of the Apocalypse may or may not be an individual—Nero or some future anti-Christ—and while symbolizing the Roman Empire, at that time in its full strength, doubtless signifies world-dominion, not in the sense of conquest, but as a formidable antagonist of the church.

Rev. A. H. Baldinger, D. D., in his suggestive treatise, "Sermons on Revelation," confirms this interpretation of the symbolic character and mission of the beast from the sea, saying: "The beast, therefore, represents primarily the political power of Rome. It just as truly represents any other political power or civil government in any age that sets itself defiantly against the Kingdom of Truth and persecutes the followers of Christ. The sea-born beast was Egypt in Moses' day, or Babylon in Isaiah's and Jeremiah's day. It was the government of Antiochus Epiphanes in the days of the Maccabees. It was Rome in John's day, Spain in the days of the Inquisition, the government of Mary in the days of John Knox, the Roman hierarchy in the days of Huss and Zwingle and Luther. It is Turkey in our own day."

Not always, however, does the beast function in the form of a world-kingdom or persecuting political power. In a still wider sense his spirit lives in what is known in present nomenclature as "worldliness." Christ was assailed under this form. "All the kingdoms of the world" were claimed by Satan and offered Christ upon condition of "worship"—adopting worldly conformity and worldly methods. Christ refused the compromise and chose His crown by way of the cross. The church and the Christian can triumph over the beast only in the same way. It is said of others "they worshipped the dragon, which gave power unto the beast." Rev. 13:4—exactly what Satan demanded of Christ.

Scholars and Christian writers in all ages have differed as to the meaning of wounding unto death one of the heads of the beast. Possibly it signifies the fall of the Roman Empire, whose spirit still "lives" in the worldly principles actuating all human governments—antagonistic to the spiritual ideals of Christianity. To practice worldly conformity is to receive the mark of the beast—his brand in all ages. "He that leadeth into captivity shall go into captivity" is the assurrance of victory by him "that leadeth captivity captive." "Here is the patience and faith of the saints." "In the world ye shall have tribulation; but be of good cheer; I have overcome the world."—John 16:33.

The Third Enemy of the Church

The second "beast, coming up out of the earth," is the vicegerent of the first, which itself serves the dragon in the same capacity. "Two horns like a Lamb and he spake as a dragon," is sufficient to indicate his false character. His "making fire to come down from heaven and his "power to give life unto the image of the beast," must be understood not literally but in keeping with the symbolic character of the book.

In the next Cycle his character and mission are more clearly revealed, where he is identified as "the false prophet" —not Mohammed as some have thought, nor the Pope of Rome as others have insisted, nor as a matter of fact any one individual or organization. He is an ecclesiastical product, any false religion or apostate phase of Christianity, as general as worldly conformity—symbolized by the first beast —and which appears in all eras of human history.

Just as Antiochus Epiphanes, the Anti-Christ of Daniel, or the emperor, Nero, possibly the Anti-Christ of the Apocalypse, may be an individual representing the world-spirit symbolized by the first beast; so Mohammed, the Pope, Joseph Smith, Mary Baker, Eddy, Pastor Russell, may as individuals represent the false teaching symbolized by the second beast or "false prophet"; but no one individual can fulfil all of his characteristics; neither can any one ecclesiastical organization in itself exhaust all of his mission and activities.

The second beast in later Cycles appears in a twofold capacity, one in the character of "false prophet" and the other as mystic "Babylon," the harlot. In the latter personification, it is Apostate Christianity exclusively that is represented—just one phase of the mission of the beast. In a more comprehensive sphere the second beast as "false prophet" is Paganism, Gnosticism, Mohammedanism, Mormonism, Christian Science, Apostate Romanism, Nominal Protestantism, Judaism, Rationalism, Modernism and all the false faiths which have cursed the human race since the fall. As there have been many "false Christs," so there have been many false faiths and will be till the Second Coming and the battle of Armageddon, when the beast and the false prophet will be conquered and cast into the bottomless pit, whence they came.

The Interdict

The interdict "that no man might buy or sell, save he that had the mark . . . of the beast," has been fulfilled time again. "Christians who renounced their faith and embraced Emperor Worship were given "stigmata," metal checks or marks on the body, which were the signs of their apostasy and gave immunity from persecution. Those who refused to burn incense to the emperor were disfranchised politically, ostracized socially, and boycotted commercially. Like the early Christians in Jerusalem, they could neither buy in the open market nor sell. They were deprived of the very means of livelihood. If social and economic pressure failed to accomplish its purpose, sterner methods were adopted. They were exiled to die in the mountains or on distant islands of the sea; they were thrown to wild beasts; nailed to crosses and tormented by every means that could be conceived in devil-possessed brains. The civil authority and the religious authority of the empire were, therefore, united in a common effort to crush the followers of the Nazarene, to annihiliate the church.

"While the earth-born beast to John's mind represented Caesar worship, it represents just as well any religion that is created or controlled by the state and used by the state to promote its own temporal ends. . . . And wherever and whenever a Pagan government and a Christless church have been merged under one head and controlled by one authority; wherever church and state have been married, the results have always been similar to those John describes, the degradation of both church and state, irresponsible autocracy and the perpetration of fearful injustices. This combine of beastly powers, the joining of civil and religious authority in one hand, reached its devilish climax in the tenth and thirteenth centuries when carnal popes arrogated to themselves the title of "God's vicegerent on earth." Innocent III believed that as successor to Peter, Christ had given him authority not only over the church, but over the entire world of human affairs. . . .

"Therefore, the right to trample on the necks of kings was his by divine prerogative. The lives of men, the crowns of kings, the destinies of nations, were in his hand. Princes, states and parliaments were obliged to bring their differences to him for adjudication. He made and unmade kings and kingdoms at will. In order to enforce his decrees and to compel the world to bow to his will, he inaugurated the Inquisition, a hell-born institution, which almost crushed truth from the earth."—Sermons on Revelation, pp. 136, 137.

Missionaries have reported that wherever converts have forsaken false faiths they have been persecuted, their business ruined and themselves driven from community to community by their relentless foes. The Turk is not the sole offender. Romanism, wherever it has possessed civil power, and churches established and supported by the state, have laid grievous interdicts on Non-Conformists. Worldly conformity and worldly methods have also often been the price of success by those willing to pay the price—the mark of the beast.

"Six Hundred and Threescore and Six"

In its essential character the Apocalypse is intensely symbolic. Numbers can no more be taken in a literal sense than can "beasts," "locusts," "frogs," etc. Our present Arabic numerals were not in force at the time John lived, and as he wrote in Greek he must have used the method of the times, wherein each letter in this alphabet had a numerical value.

By reason of this fact, the number of the beast, "six hundred threescore and six," has been used as a Cryptogram and applied to every individual, supposed by any interpreter to fulfil its hidden meaning, where the numerical value of the letters total six hundred and sixty-six.

The following is an illustration of this type of interpretation. The title "Lateinos"—the Latin one—has been taken as the significant term for the Roman Empire; and its letters used as numerals total 666. L=30, a=1, t=300, e=5, i=10, n=50, o=70 and s=200—total 666. Canon Farrar and others have undertaken to make the application to Nero as the beast; but in order to do so, it is necessary to use the Hebrew form, "Neron Caesar"; and, singularly enough, the Hebrew letters are equivalent to 666. Gabbardt suggests that both "Lateinos" and "Neron Caesar" were intended to be concealed under this name by John, who thus indicates that the Roman Empire and Nero are alike symbolized as the beast.

The Seventh Day Adventists, leading all others in fanciful interpretations, contend that it signifies the Pope—using the numerical equivalents of the expression, "the vicar of the Son of God." The Catholics have returned the compliment by applying it to Martin Luther, or others of the reformers. By shrewd manipulation it has been made to fit numerous individuals such as Diocletian, Titus, Vespasian, Julian the Apostate, Mohammed, Napoleon and Kaisar William. All such efforts to solve the mystery of the number of the beast have always proven unsatisfactory, unprofitable and misleading.

It is exceedingly doubtful if it stands for any specific individual. Some have given it a symbolical interpretation in the following form: As the number seven is the Jewish symbol of perfection, so the number six would signify *almost but failure.* Consequently the number six hundred and sixty-six would thrice emphasize that fact, suggesting seeming triumph for a time, or else signal failure at the very moment that success was all but assured.

The special object of this Cycle is to reveal the great enemies of the church. Satan is chief, above and outside of the church—a malicious personal spirit, the destroyer, analogue of Christ the Savior. The first beast is "the world," which surrounds the church—the spirit of the age—against which John elsewhere warns: "Love not the world, neither the things that are in the world. If any man love the world, the love of the Father is not in him."—I John 3:15. The second beast, called elsewhere "The False Prophet," is the rival of the church, sometimes within the fold itself—falsehood similating the truth—designated by Paul as "another gospel, which is not another." The individual Christian faces the same three enemies in his spiritual warfare and must "resist the devil," "be not conformed to this world," and must struggle against "the flesh."

The Interlude

In this Cycle the Interlude occurs just before the end of the age with its catastrophe of judgments. The design is the same. In exhibiting these powerful enemies, the Apocalypse, true to its purpose of revealing conflict and yet the preservation of the saints, hastens to furnish the "consolation." In the very presence of these powerful and inveterate foes, the church is assured of absolute safety.

Reverting to former Cycles, after the opening "Seals" had revealed "the great day of wrath," and before the trumpets sound their awful judgments upon the world, the hand of the angel is stayed in their execution till God's servants "one hundred and forty and four thousand"—mystic number—are sealed and thereby rendered immune from the impending "woes." Now here again, with the dragon raging against them, the beast persecuting and the false prophet seducing, the one hundred and forty and four thousand appear calmly standing on Mount Zion with the Lamb, as complete as before—not one missing—"having his Father's name written in their foreheads" rendering them inviolable. Not only are they safe, but they are singing the anthem of redemption—"a new song before the throne . . . and no man could learn that song, but the one hundred and forty and four thousand, which were redeemed from the earth." The song is unrecorded, but the theme is redemption and safety and victory.

Heralds of the Approaching End

This chorus of the redeemed is supplemented by angelic heralds, following each in quick succession, celebrating the final triumph of the Gospel and the approaching end of the age. This is a new feature introduced in this Cycle in keeping with the plan and structure of the Apocalypse—elaborating each time more fully the dramatic circumstances characterizing the close of the Dispensation.

The first angel is seen "flying in the midst of heaven, having the everlasting Gospel to preach unto them that dwell on the earth, and to every nation, and kindred, and tongue and people, saying with a loud voice,

> Fear God and give glory to him;
> For the hour of his judgment is come:
> And worship him that made heaven,
> And earth and the sea and fountains of water."

The Gospel flying on the wings of an angel in the last days, indicating the revival of missionary zeal and activity, parallels the statement of Christ: "This gospel of the kingdom shall be preached in all the world for a witness to all nations; and then shall the end come." It is one of the signs of the times being strikingly fulfilled before our eyes, which is more in evidence than doubtful calculations based upon questionable data as to the exact date of the approaching Second Coming.

The second angel followed immediately, saying, "Babylon is fallen, is fallen, that great city, because she made all nations drink of the wine of the wrath of her fornication." The fall of Babylon, mentioned here for the first time, will be more fully elaborated in the remaining Cycles—in accordance with the arrangements of the unfolding plan, first the hint in one vision and then the dramatic description in the next—another one of the signs of the times indicating the approaching end.

The third angel followed them, saying with a loud voice, "If any man worship the beast and his image, and receive his mark in his forehead, or in his hand, the same shall drink of the wine of the wrath of God, which is poured out without mixture into the cup of his indignation. . . . Here is the patience of the saints: here are they that keep the commandments of God and the faith of Jesus." This is the final warning of the beginning of the end.

Solo of Consolation

Now follows "a voice from heaven saying unto me, write:

> Blessed are the dead
> Which die in the Lord from henceforth:
> Yea, saith the Spirit,
> That they may rest from their labors;
> And their works do follow them."

The significance of this obscure text with which the Interlude concludes, just as the Dispensation is about to close, is not entirely apparent. The consolation therein contained was perhaps more clearly apprehended by that generation of Christians than those of succeeding ages. The following is suggested as a plausible interpretation:

Death has always been to saint and sinner alike the most dreaded enemy, the king of terrors; and the saintliest soul of earth needs sustaining grace, and the comfort of the most precious promises, as well as the everlasting arms underneath, as his feet sink in the cold waters and the waves and billows roll over him "in the swellings of Jordan." The consolation of this assurance of blessedness has a double application, not only sustaining the faith of the dying saint, but affording the most soothing comfort to the bereaved, whose hearts are torn with anguish at the loss of those dearer than life itself.

However, in the apostolic age, as already suggested, this assurance meant more than to any succeeding generation. In the early days of Christianity the saints were regaled with the most sacred memories of Jesus, by many of His contemporaries still living, and were thrilled with anticipations of His near return and the joy of welcoming Him as the Deliverer in the days of the bitter persecutions. To those facing the executioner's block or other forms of martyrdom, what could be more re-assuring in their disappointment than the precious words, "Blessed are the dead which die in the Lord"—doubtless suggested as sufficient compensation for the dreaded fagot and flame. In his early ministry the writer was associated with a venerable Baptist minister, a veritable saint on earth. On one occasion he asked this aged servant of God, "Would it not be a glorious thing to be one of the number who never die, but were alive to meet the Lord at His coming?" To which he characteristically replied: "Yes; but I would not like to be kept out of heaven one moment even to avoid death and to be among the number to welcome Him at His coming." This incident may serve to throw light on the significance of the consolation to those early Christians, who were thus assured that death was an immediate passport to glory, and to the rest that remaineth to the people of God.

The End of the Age

The Cycle now ends, as the previous visions did, with the same cataclysmic convulsions of nature and world harvest in the spiritual realm of being:

"And I looked, and behold a white cloud, and upon the cloud one sat like unto the Son of man, having on his head a golden crown, and in his hand a sharp sickle. And another angel came out of the temple, crying with a loud voice to him that sat on the cloud, Thrust in thy sickle, and reap: for the time is come for thee to reap; for the harvest of the earth is ripe. And he that sat on the cloud thrust in his sickle on the earth; and the earth was reaped."

This language interprets itself, announcing not only the Second Coming, but the purpose of it to reap the harvest of earth. In all probability this was the gathering of "his own"—the wheat into the barn—by Christ before the next event.

"And another angel came out of the temple which is in heaven, he also having a sharp sickle. And another angel came out from the altar, which had power over fire; and cried with a loud cry to him that had the sharp sickle, saying, "Thrust in thy sharp sickle, and gather the clusters of the vine of the earth; for her grapes are fully ripe.

"And the angel thrust in his sickle into the earth, and gathered the vine of the earth, and cast it into the great winpress of the wrath of God. And the winepress was trodden without the city, and the blood came out of the winepress, even unto the horse bridles, by the space of a thousand and six hundred furlongs." This was doubtless the harvest of the wicked tares after Christ had claimed his own.

This account of the End is strikingly similar to that described by Christ Himself and recorded in Matt. 13:39-43:

"The harvest is the end of the world; and the reapers are the angels. As, therefore, the tares are gathered and burned in the fire; so shall it be in the end of this world. The Son of man shall send forth his angels, and they shall gather out of his kingdom all things that offend, and them which do iniquity; and shall cast them into a furnace of fire: there shall be wailing and gnashing of teeth. Then shall the righteous shine forth as the sun in the kingdom of their Father. Who hath ears to hear, let him hear."

The agreement of Scripture with Scripture is the proof of its credibility. It is self-evidencing. The close of each Cycle with the same judgment scene is incontestable evidence that the Apocalypse is not composed of vague, rambling, incoherent visions, but written with a perfect plan and purpose, growing more and more apparent each moment, and still more strikingly confirmed by every comparison of its component parts.

The FIFTH CYCLE

TEXT: CHAPTERS XV-XVI

John: "And I saw another sign in heaven, great and marvelous, seven angels, having the seven last plagues; for in them is filled up the wrath of God. And I saw as it were a sea of glass mingled with fire: and them that had gotten the victory over the beast, and over his image, and over his mark, and over the number of his name, stand on the sea of glass, having the harps of God. And they sing the song of Moses, the servant of God, and the song of the Lamb, saying,

Victorious Hosts: "Great and marvelous are thy works, Lord God Almighty;
Just and true are thy ways, thou King of saints.
Who shall not fear thee, O Lord
And glorify thy name?
For thou art holy:
For all nations shall come and worship before thee.
For thy judgments are made manifest." . . .

John: "And the seven angels came out of the temple, having the seven plagues, clothed in pure and white linen, and having their breasts girded with golden girdles. And one of the four beasts gave unto the seven angeles seven golden vials full of the wrath of God, who liveth for ever and ever. . . . And I heard a great voice out of the temple saying to the seven angeles, Go your ways, and pour out the vials of the wrath of God upon the earth." . . .

Voice from the Altar: "Even so, Lord God Almighty, true and righteous are thy judgments."

John: "And the sixth angel poured out his vial upon the great river Euphrates; and the water thereof was dried up, that the way of the kings of the east might be prepared.
"And I saw three unclean spirits like frogs come out of the mouth of the dragon, and out of the mouth of the beast, and out of the mouth of the false prophet. For they are the spirits of devils, working miracles, which go forth unto the kings of the earth and of the whole world, to gather them to the battle of that great day of God Almighty."

Jesus: "Behold, I come as a thief. Blessed is he that watcheth, and keepeth his garments, lest he walk naked, and they see his shame."

John: "And he gathered them together into a place called in the Hebrew tongue Armageddon. And the seventh angel poured out his vial into the air; and there came a great voice out of the temple of heaven, from the throne, saying, It is done.
"And there were voices, and thunders, and lightnings; and there was a great earthquake, such as was not since men were upon the earth, so mighty an earthquake and so great. And the great city was divided into three parts, and the cities of the nations fell: and great Babylon came in remembrance before God, to give unto her the cup of the wine of the fierceness of his wrath. And every island fled away, and the mountains were not found. And there fell upon men a great hail out of heaven, every stone about the weight of a talent: and men blasphemed God because of the plague of the hail: for the plague thereof was exceeding great."

CHAPTER VII

The SEVEN VIALS—JUDGMENTS ON APOSTACY

THE fifth Cycle, embracing Chapters XV-XVI, presents the vision of the seven angels with "the seven last plagues," pouring out the Vials of divine wrath upon offenders, thereby revealing the judgments upon Apostacy. The term, "Vials," is used as in the authorized version, although "bowls" or "censers" would perhaps more correctly describe the vessels of wrath. The censer, containing incense pleasing unto God, may be thus transformed into a vessel of wrath charged with the judgments of God.

Trumpets vs. Vials

The similarity and contrast between the Trumpets of the third Cycle and Vials of the fifth are very striking. In the first case the church is in the world, and the judgments fall in full severity upon the ungodly world. In the second case the world is in the church, and the latter is the object of the divine wrath for its fearful Apostacy.

It must be kept well in mind, that while the Cycles themsleves are synchronous and each presents in turn the Christian Dispensation, yet the events of each are not necessarily strictly parallel. In other words, some may cover the whole period of the particular Cycle. In others the emphasis may be laid on events taking place near the beginning of the Dispensation, while others still may devote attention chiefly to occurrences at its close; but all the Cycles without exception coincide in describing the end of the age. As the Vials are represented as containing "the seven last plagues," it would be reasonable to infer that this panorama presents events taking place largely toward the close, after Apostacy had corrupted the church.

The correspondence between the Trumpets and Vials being so remarkable, this would seem to be the proper place to reenforce the main contention of this interpretation, that each Cycle or panorama is co-extensive with the Christian Dispensation.

Tables of Comparison

The following table prepared by Prof. Milligan reveals this parallelism more forcefully than any elaborate argument possible can:

	TRUMPETS	VIALS
	Relating to	*Relating to*
First.	The earth, Chap. viii. 7.	The earth, Chap. xvi. 2.
Second.	The sea, Chap. viii. 8.	The sea, Chap. xvi. 3.
Third.	Rivers and fountains of the waters, Chap. viii. 10.	Rivers and fountains of the waters, Chap. xvi. 4.
Fourth.	The sun and moon and stars, Chap. viii. 12.	The sun, Chap. xvi. 8.
Fifth.	The pit of the abyss, Chap. ix. 2.	The throne of the beast, Chap. xvi. 10.
Sixth.	The great river Euphrates, Chap. ix. 14.	The great river Euphrates, Chap. xvi. 12.
Seventh.	Great voices in heaven, followed by lightnings, and voices, and thunders, and an earthquake, and great hail, Chap. xi. 15-19.	A great voice from the throne, followed by lightnings, and voices, and thunders, a great earthquake, and great hail. Chap. xvi. 17-18-21.

In his treatise on Prophecy the late Principal Fairburn supports this interpretation most conclusively:

"It is surely, against all reasonable probability, to suppose that these two lines of symbolic representation, touching at so many points, alike in their commencement, their progress, and their termination, can relate to dispensations of providence wholly unconnected, and to periods of time separated from one another by the lapse of ages. It is immeasurably more probable that they are but different aspects of substantially the same course of procedure, different merely from the parties subjected to it being contemplated in somewhat different relations. Nor would it be possible, if two entire series of symbolical delineations following so nearly in the same track were yet to point to events quite remote and diverse, to vindicate such delineations from the charge of arbitrariness and indetermination."

Dr. Marion McH. Hull, Bible student of Atlanta, Ga., and Expositor of the Syndicated International Sunday-school Lessons, has prepared a table equally valuable, re-enforcing the synchronous theory of the Cycles—with which the author thoroughly agrees, except as to the symbolic meaning of the rider on "the white horse," it being his interpretation that the rider is the conquering Christ Himself:

"Naturally we think that the seals were opened one after another, that then the trumpets were blown one after another, and that then the Vials were poured out one after another. But careful study shows that this is not the case. They are neither consecutive nor simultaneous, but they are parallel. They are like a series of dissolving views; or more like a picture as it is drawn—first the general outlines, then a bit more detail, then the finishing touches until the whole is completed. Each traces the course of divine action up to the grand consummation."

SEALS	TRUMPETS	VIALS
1. White Horse—Victorious False Christs.	1. Hail and Fire, ⅓ trees.	1. Grievous sore on beast worshippers.
2. Red Horse—Sword.	2. Burning Mt., ⅓ sea, etc.	2. Sea, Blood.
3. Black Horse—Famine.	3. Star, ⅓ rivers.	3. Rivers and fountains, blood.
4. Pale Horse—Death.	4. ⅓ sun, ⅓ moon, ⅓ stars. (Therefore prior to 6th seal.)	4. Sun scorches impenitent.
5. Martyrs Cry for Vengeance.	5. Locusts and their king torment all but sealed of God. (Therefore, after 6th seal.)	5. On throne of beast.
6. Earthquake—Lord's Coming ushered in with terrors to ungodly. Sun black, mighty phenomena. Episode— Elect of Israel sealed. Elect of Gentile sealed.	6. 4 angels loosed to kill ⅓ men. Episodse of ch. 10-14, Harvest. Vintage.	6. Euphrates dried up. Armageddon. Episode—The three frog-like spirits.
7. Angel in heaven answers prayer of martyrs. Fire from altar on earth. Thunderings, etc., usher in final consummation.	7. Temple opened in heaven. Thanksgiving for answered prayer. Altar seen. Christ's Kingdom established. Thunderings, etc.	7. Final consummation — Voice in heaven saying, It is done. Thunderings, earthquakes, etc.

While it is somewhat in anticipation of things to come, perhaps it would be advisable to incorporate here the author's comparison, substantiating his conclusion by exhibiting the details of the Judgment Scene common to all these visions:

First Cycle: The Second Coming, The Marriage Supper.
Rev. 3:20-21 The Reign of Christ and the Saints.

Second Cycle: Earthquake. Sun, Moon, and Stars Smitten.
Rev. 6:12-17 Heavens departing as a scroll.
Mountains and islands removed.
The Great Day of Wrath.

Third Cycle: Rev. 11:15-19	The Reign of Christ. The wrath of God. Lightnings, thunderings, earthquake and great hail. The Judgment of the Dead.
Fourth Cycle: Rev. 14:14-20	The Second Coming. Harvest of the world reaped. Winepress of the Wrath of God.
Fifth Cycle: Rev. 16:15-21	Second Coming. Armageddon. Thunders, lightnings, earthquake. Fall of Babylon. Islands and mountains removed. Great Hail. Cup of Wine of the fierceness of Wrath.
Sixth Cycle: Rev. 19:11-21	Second Coming. Armageddon. Winepress of the Fierceness and Wrath of Almighty God. Lake of Fire.
Seventh Cycle: Rev. 20:7-21	Armageddon. Resurrection. Reign of Christ. Judgment of the Dead. Lake of Fire.

Upon comparing these seven conclusions, if they do not describe the same Judgment Scene at the close of the Dispensation, it would seem almost impossible to interpret human language. They furnish irresistible proof that these seven Cycles are synchronous, covering the present Dispensation, each terminating with the end of the age.

The Interlude

In this Cycle the Interlude is at the beginning of the panorama. In the first two the Interlude with its Chorus of Consolation came after the close. In the third it was synchronous and coincided with the Judgment Scene. In the fourth it came just before the end. Now in the fifth it occurs at the beginning before the judgments fall. While this arrangement seems to interrupt the structural plan of the book, it is what Milligan terms "it's law of a higher symmetry." In this particular case the consolation is furnished God's children beforehand to fortify them for the awful judgments about to fall upon the Apostate Church.

The setting of the stage for the Interlude opens to view an entrancing scene in heaven:

"And I saw as it were a sea of glass mingled with fire: and them that had gotten the victory over the beast, and over his image, and over his mark, and over the number of his name, stand on the sea of glass, having the harps of God. And they sing the song of Moses, the servant of God, and the song of the Lamb, saying,

> "Great and marvelous are thy works, Lord God Almighty:
> Just and true arc thy way, thou King of Saints.
> Who shall not fear thee, O Lord,
> And glorify thy name?
> For thou art holy:
> For all nations shall come
> And worship before thee;
> For thy Judgments are made manifest."

This Chorus of the Redeemed sings consolation and courage to the saints of earth about to be subjected to the fearful "seven last plagues," imminent, ready to descend in terrible force upon the Apostate Church, guaranteeing inferentially immunity to the faithful in the midst of the fiery trial which will finally sift the wheat from the tares.

The pouring out of the Vials of wrath follows strictly the same order in the realms affected as did the sounding of the Trumpets—the first in each series affecting "the earth"; the second in each "the sea"; the third in each "the rivers and fountains of waters"; and so throughout the series. They each have some special symbolic or spiritual significance, the consideration of which is not, however, within the scope of this study and must therefore be passed by to pursue the purpose involved in this interpretation.

Distinctive Features Added

This fifth Cycle, like all the others, repeats and magnifies the occurrences which were mere hints in previous panoramas, and then adds new features which likewise are destined to be more fully elaborated in succeeding visions—each being a clearer revelation of the purpose of God. The special features added are two: 1—The "False Prophet"—identified, however, as the second beast. 2—The Battle of Armageddon—the final conflict between Christ and Satan, leading their respective hosts of good and evil.

The False Prophet

The identification of the false prophet with the second beast is unmistakable as shown: (1)—by his character described in Rev. 13:11 as having "two horns like a lamb" and yet speaking "as a dragon"—the very personification of falsehood: (2)—by his office, "causeth the earth and them which dwell therein to worship the first beast . . . and deceiveth them that dwell on the earth"—the unmistakable practice of falsehood: (3)—by the two being used *synonymously* in the following enumeration of the Trinity of Evil:

> "And I saw three unclean spirits like frogs come out of the mouth of the *dragon,* and out of the mouth of the *beast,* and out of the mouth of the *false prophet.* For they are the spirits of devils, working miracles, which go forth unto the kings of the earth and of the whole world, to gather them to the battle of that great day of God Almighty."

In this highly symbolical book, must we take this language in a strictly literal sense? Were these "three unclean spirits like frogs" distinct personalities? Is not the statement that they came out of the mouths of the dragon, beast and false prophet highly significant? Does not this language find its counterpart in the statement, that upon the Second Coming of Christ, "out his mouth goeth a sharp sword, that with it he should smite the nations"?—Rev. 19:15. Are we not justified in interpreting these unclean spirits therefore as the false teaching of the Trinity of Evil?

Armageddon

Introduced for the first time in this fifth Cycle, to be more fully elaborated and minutely narrated in the next two, Armageddon—designated as "the battle of that great day of God Almighty"—is highly significant. It means literally "the hill of Megiddo," situated on the plain of Erdraelon, the historic battlefield of the ages. Here Sisera was defeated by Barak—Judges 5:19; here the Midianites were defeated by Gideon—Judges 7; King Saul, defeated by the Philistines —I Samuel 28:4; and afterward Josiah, defeated by Pharaoh Necho—II Kings 23:29-30. It was also the battleground between Napoleon Bonaparte and the Turks. The gathering of "Gog" and "Magog" prophesied in the thirty-eighth Chapter of Ezekiel and recorded in Rev. 20:8 is either identical with, or elses the type of, Armageddon.

Is this last great conflict of the ages to be interpreted in a literal or symbolic sense? If he, whose "name is called the Word of God," shall smite his enemies with the sword which "goeth out of his mouth," and if the Word of God is elsewhere identified as "the Sword of the Spirit," does not this suggest that Armageddon signifies the last supreme effort of Satan and his hosts, a spiritual conflict? It is true that it is spoken of as "a place called in the Hebrew tongue Armageddon"; but does this signify anything more than a historic place of many defeats, just as if we should speak of it as the battle in which Satan meets his final "Waterloo"?

It is highly significant that in the very midst of announcing Armageddon occurs a parenthetical clause: "Behold, I come as a thief—unexpectedly—Blessed is he that watcheth!" Later in Chapter XIX, in connection with Armageddon, we have the most elaborate description in all Scripture of the Second Coming of Christ. Does not this plainly indicate that at the very moment Satan makes his greatest rally and most impressive array of forces—consisting of false faiths, rationalists, modernists, and blatant scoffers—Christ will suddenly appear as a thief in the night and utterly and eternally overwhelm the combined world-forces of evil?

What are the ominous "signs of the times" today? Does this Laodicean age of indifference, combined with the rally everywhere throughout the world against the truth and the prevalent tendency to rebel against divine authority, indicate that the crisis is at hand? Are we already in the midst of the great spiritual Armageddon of prophecy? Do all these things point to the near approach of the Son of God?

The Final Consummation

"And the seventh angel poured out his Vial into the air; and there came a great voice out of the temple of heaven, from the throne, saying, It is done." Does not this hark back to the third Cycle just before "the seventh angel sounded," when a mighty angel standing, one foot on the sea and the other on the earth, "swore by him that liveth forever and ever . . . that there should be time no longer"—literally no further delay? On the cross, Christ, "with a loud voice," uttered as His last word, "Tetelesthai," translated "It is finished"; and now "from the throne" "a great voice" announces, "It is done."

Then follows the same Judgment Scene, convulsions of nature, thunders and lightnings and a great earthquake, the fall of Babylon and "the cup of the wine of the fierceness of his wrath" for the ungodly and defiant forces of wickedness.

The curtain again drops. The Dispensation is ended.

The SIXTH CYCLE

TEXT: CHAPTERS XVII-XVIII-XIX

John: "And there came one of the seven angels which had the seven vials, and talked with me, saying unto me,

Angel: "Come hither; I will shew unto thee the judgment of the great whore that sitteth upon many waters: with whom the kings of the earth have committed fornication, and the inhabitants of the earth have been made drunk with the wine of her fornication."

John: "So he carried me away in the spirit into the wilderness; and I saw a woman sit upon a scarlet coloured beast, full of names of blasphemy, having seven heads and ten horns.
"And the woman was arrayed in purple and scarlet colour, and decked with gold and precious stones and pearls, having a golden cup in her hand full of abominations and filthiness of her fornication: and upon her forehead was a name written, MYSTERY, BABYLON THE GREAT, THE MOTHER OF HARLOTS AND ABOMINATIONS OF THE EARTH. And I saw the woman drunken with the blood of the saints, and with the blood of the martyrs of Jesus: and when I saw her, I wondered with great admiration. And the angel said unto me,

Angel: "Wherefore didst thou marvel? I will tell thee the mystery of the woman, and of the beast that carrieth her, which hath the seven heads and ten horns.
"The beast that thou sawest was, and is not; and shall ascend out of the bottomless pit, and go into perdition: and they that dwell on the earth shall wonder, whose names were not written in the book of life from the foundation of the world, when they behold the beast that was, and is not, and yet is. And here is the mind which hath wisdom. The seven heads are seven mountains, on which the woman sitteth. And there are seven kings: five are fallen, and one is, and the other is not yet come; and when he cometh, he must continue a short space. And the beast that was, and is not, even he is the eighth, and is of the seven, and goeth into perdition. And the ten horns which thou sawest are ten kings, which have received no kingdom as yet; but receive power as kings one hour with the beast.

"These have one mind, and shall give their power and strength unto the beast. These shall make war with the Lamb, and the Lamb shall overcome them: for he is Lord of lords, and King of kings: and they that are with him are called, and chosen, and faithful.

"And he saith unto me, The waters which thou sawest, where the whore sitteth, are peoples, and multitudes, and nations, and tongues. And the ten horns which thou sawest upon the beast, these shall hate the whore, and shall make her desolate and naked, and shall eat her flesh, and burn her with fire." . . .

John: "And after these things I saw another angel come down from heaven, having great power; and the earth was lightened with his glory. And he cried mightily with a strong voice, saying,

Mighty Angel: "Babylon the great is fallen, is fallen, and is become the habitation of devils, and the hold of every foul spirit, and a cage of every unclean and hateful bird. For all nations have drunk of the wine of the wrath of her fornication, and the kings of the earth have committed fornication with her, and the merchants of the earth are waxed rich through the abundance of her delicacies." . . .

Voice from Heaven: "Come out of her, my people, that ye be not partakers of her sins, and that ye receive not of her plagues. For her sins have reached unto heaven, and God hath remembered her iniquities. Reward her even as she rewarded you, and double unto her double according to her works: in the cup which she hath filled, fill to her double.

"How much she hath glorified herself, and lived deliciously, so much torment and sorrow give her: for she saith in her heart, I sit a queen and am no widow, and shall see no sorrow. Therefore, shall her plagues come in one day, death, and mourning, and famine; and she shall be utterly burned with fire: for strong is the Lord God who judgeth her." . . .

Heavenly Hosts: "Alleluia; Salvation, and glory, and honour, and power, unto the Lord our God: for true and righteous are his judgments: for he hath judged the great whore, which did corrupt the earth with her fornication, and hath avenged the blood of his servants at her hand. And again they said, Alleluia." . . .

Four and Twenty Elders: "Amen; Alleluia."

Voice from Throne: "Praise our God, all ye his servants, and ye that fear him, both small and great." . . .

Vast Multitude: "Alleluia: for the Lord God omnipotent reigneth. Let us be glad and rejoice, and give honour to him; for the

marriage of the Lamb is come, and his wife hath made herself ready.
"And to her was granted that she should be arrayed in fine linen, clean and white: for the fine linen is the righteousness of saints. Blessed are they which are called unto the marriage supper of the Lamb." . . .

John: "And I saw heaven opened, and behold a white horse; and he that sat upon him was called Faithful and True, and in righteousness he doth judge and make war. His eyes were as a flame of fire, and on his head were many crowns; and he had a name written, that no man knew, but he himself. And he was clothed with a vesture dipped in blood: and his name is called The Word of God.
"And the armies which were in heaven followed him upon white horses, clothed in fine linen, white and clean. And out of his mouth goeth a sharp sword, that with it he should smite the nations; and he shall rule them with a rod of iron: and he treadeth the winepress of the fierceness and wrath of Almighty God. And he hath on his vesture and on his thigh a name written, KING OF KINGS, AND LORD OF LORDS. And I saw an angel standing in the sun; and he cried with a loud voice, saying, to all the fowls that fly in the midst of heaven, . . .

Angel in the Sun: "Come and gather yourselves together unto the supper of the great God; that ye may eat the flesh of kings, and the flesh of captains, and the flesh of mighty men, and the flesh of horses, and of them that sit on them, and the flesh of all men, both free and bond, both small and great."

John: "And I saw the beast, and the kings of the earth, and their armies, gathered together to make war against him that sat on the horse, and against his army.
"And the beast was taken, and with him the false prophet that wrought miracles before him, with which he deceived them that had received the mark of the beast, and them that worshipped his image. These both were cast alive into a lake of fire burning with brimstone.
"And the remnant were slain with the sword of him that sat upon the horse, which sword proceeded out of his mouth: and all the fowls were filled with their flesh."

CHAPTER VIII

DOOM *of the* SATANIC ALLIES

ONCE again in the Drama of Christianity the present Dispensation is presented in a new aspect. The panorama in this sixth Cycle deals almost exclusively with the closing scenes—the consummation of the age. The end has been reached each time, but now it is put under a microscope, and the events hinted heretofore are magnified into full proportions and described in dramatic terms. In the previous visions these details were but faint shadows of the awful reality now graphically and luridly presented.

Specific Purpose

It is a chapter of dooms. Its distinctive purpose is to represent the judgment of the allied forces of evil. The beast, the false prophet, the harlot Babylon—apostacy—all come to their doom in the final recokning at the consummation of the age, described in figurative language, which lays under tribute every human expression and power of the imagination to do justice to the subject in the effort to visualize the doom awaiting the allies of evil.

Previous judgments had been unavailing in their purpose to check wickedness. Now final judgment and doom coincide, but the effect on the impenitent is exactly the same as in preliminary visitations of wrath upon ungodliness—always ineffectual. The record of results in the following statement parallels past experiences: "They gnawed their tongues for pain and blasphemed the God of heaven because of their pains and their sores; *and repented not of their deeds."* Impenitent to the very last, which can lead only and inevitably to doom! Divine patience is at length exhausted. The axe falls. If the incorrigible were released from hell and given "another chance," would the result presumably be at all different? The effect of the loosing of Satan—whether literally or figuratively interpreted—resulting in wicked and wilful rebellion against divine government is highly significant of the immutable character of wickedness at every opportunity to express itself in overt act.

The panorama in this act of the Drama deals almost exclusively with the doom of the beast and with the judgment of the second beast, designated according to its dual character, "the false prophet," and the harlot, "Babylon," corresponding to the two prevalent types of religious fraud—false faiths and apostacy.

Delineation of Characters

This involves correct analysis. In order to any clear understanding of the Apocalypse, it is absolutely essential in any interpretation of its symbolism to assign the "dramatis personae" their unvarying significance, and to define their distinctive relations to each other and the definite parts they perform in the Drama. For example, the first and second beasts never change places nor functions. The "harlot" and "Babylon" being identified as a composite character by the inspired narrator—Rev. 17:4-6—must not be assigned different roles in any interpretation of their function. This delineation of character can be more effectively exhibited by means of the following diagram than by definitions and distinctions:

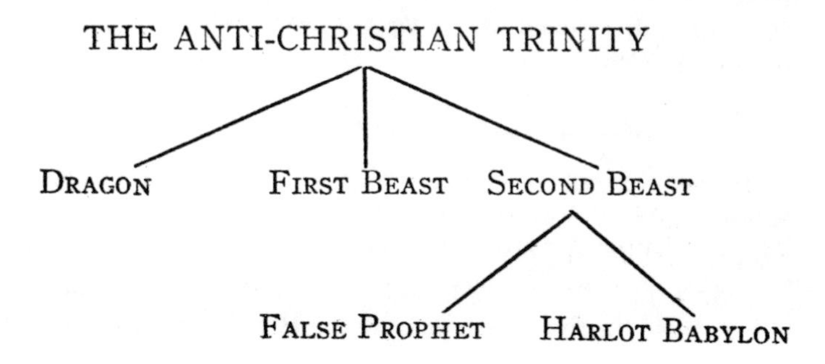

In the Holy Trinity, God the Father, is the synonym of righteousness—opposed by Satan—dragon—the embodiment of wickedness. God the Son is the synonym of Redemption—opposed by the first beast, whose function is enslavement—Rev. 13:7-10. God, the Holy Spirit, is the Revealer of divine Truth—John 16:13—opposed by the second beast in the guise of false prophet; the very symbol of falsehood.

In identifying the parties it is needless to dwell further on the dragon, "that old serpent called the devil and Satan." The first beast has been so minutely described in Rev. XIII as to leave no doubt that it is the symbol of world-domination and worldly principles.

Dual Character of the Second Beast

It requires far more skill and careful discrimination in dealing with the functions and symbolism of the second beast by reason of its dual character. After being introduced in the fourth Cycle as the beast "out of the earth," it is characterized in the next Cycle as "the false prophet." While in this sixth Cycle, it re-appears in a feminine character as the harlot, upon whose brow is written, "Mystery, Babylon the Great, the mother of harlots." Though it functions in a dual capacity, its mission is one—the establishment of falsehood in the place of truth. This dual capacity is not incidental but tremendously significant, as will be evident from the further study of its twofold character—masculine as false prophet and feminine as the harlot Babylon—the masterpiece of Satan, far more effective perhaps than any other satanic agency of evil.

1—The Beast as False Prophet

In his masculine character as false prophet he covers the whole field of falsehood in the spiritual realm—plying his satanic art to supplant the truth of God. Every Pagan religion, which substitutes idolatry for divine worship, and all other false faiths—Confucianism, Buddhism, Mohammedanism, Mormonism, Christian Science, Theosophy, Russellism, Spiritualism—are the "unclean spirits like frogs," which come "out of the mouth of the false prophet."

2—The Beast as Babylon the Harlot

In the guise of the harlot there is a narrowing of the function of the beast to a specific field in the generic sphere of religious falsehood. Not in the general character of false prophet, but in the specific role as seducer, the harlot appropriately symbolizes the *false in realm of Christendom.* The harlot does not represent false faiths in general, but exclusively apostacy from spiritual Christianity. She is the most subtle foe with which the church must contend, the most repulsive to Christ of all the enemies of Christianity, and characterized as "the Great Whore."

Just as Christian Science is the most dangerous of all false faiths, because it similates Christianity, so apostacy is the deadly enemy of the church, because it is within the fold and is mistaken for Christianity—Satan's counterfeit for the church of God.

The following language is not too strong as a delineation of the character of apostacy, the enemy and rival of the "Bride, the Lamb's wife":

"And there came one of the seven angels which had the seven vials, and talked with me, saying unto me, Come hither; I will shew unto thee the judgment of the great whore that sitteth upon many waters: with whom the kings of the earth have committed fornication, and the inhabitants of the earth have been made drunk with the wine of her fornication.

"So he carried me away in the spirit into the wilderness: and I saw a woman sit upon a scarlet coloured beast, full of names of blasphemy, having seven heads and ten horns. And the woman was arrayed in purple and scarlet colour, and decked with gold and precious stones and pearls, having a golden cup in her hand full of abominations and filthiness of her fornication.

"And upon her forehead was a name written, MYSTERY, BABYLON THE GREAT, THE MOTHER OF HARLOTS AND ABOMINATIONS OF THE EARTH. And I saw the woman drunken with the blood of the saints, and with the blood of the martyrs of Jesus; and when I saw her, I wondered with great admiration."

The Harlot vs. The Bride

The harlot is the analogue or antithesis of "the bride, the Lamb's wife." It is no mixed metaphor to represent her also as "Babylon, that great city." The Bride is also represented under the metaphor of a city:

"And there came unto me one of the seven angels which had the seven vials full of the seven last plagues, and talked with me, saying, Come hither, I will shew thee the bride, the Lamb's wife. And he carried me away in the spirit to a great and high mountain, and shewed me that great city, the holy Jerusalem, descending out of heaven from God."

Is the following striking contrast merely incidental; or does it exhibit evidence of intentional purpose?

The New Jerusalem. Rev. 3:12; 21:2.	The Old Jerusalem.
The Heavenly Jerusalem. Heb. 12:22.	The Earthly Jerusalem.
The Jerusalem to come. Heb. 13:14.	The Jerusalem which now is. Gal. 4:25.
The Jerusalem which is above. Gal. 4:26.	The Jerusalem which is below.
The Jerusalem which is free. Gal. 4:26.	The Jerusalem in bondage. Gal 4:25.
The Bride. Rev. 21:2.	The Harlot. Rev. 17:1.

Corresponding to this parallel, Apostacy is "the whore," "Babylon that great city with whom the kings of the earth commit fornication." She does not wait for "the marriage of the Lamb," but "saith in her heart, I sit a queen and am no widow"—in contradistinction from the widowhood of the church during the absence of her Lord. Study carefully the original of this prophecy in Isaiah 47. The Bride, the true Church, is faithful to her marriage vow. The harlot, Apostacy, is unfaithful, committing fornication with the kings of the earth.

"Sitting upon a scarlet coloured beast," she has been mistakenly identified with apostate Roman Catholicism, which is, however, only a partial truth. In so far as Rome is apostate the description fits her case to that extent, but unfortunately apostacy is not confined to Rome. It is as wide as Christendom, and is equally chargeable against Protestantism in any fundamental departure from revealed truth as manifest in Rationalism, Modernism, Unitarianism, and other spurious forms or degenerate phases of Christianity.

Babylon, the name applied to the harlot, harks back to the Tower of Babel, one of the earliest wide-spread defections of the race in its defiance of God, vainly imagining it could erect a tower rendering it independent of divine providence. The name literally signifies "confusion," a characteristic which clings still and renders it somewhat difficult of definition in any interpretation of its symbolism.

Ecclesiastical vs. Political

In the strictly religious application of the term, ecclesiastical Babylon is a fundamental departure from the faith, corresponding somewhat to "Baal worship" on the part of ancient Israel, denounced in the Old Testament uniformly as "whoredom," and in the Apocalypse as "fornication."

Political Babylon in its varied forms represents alliance with the state or compromise with the world, whereby the spiritual character of the church is sacrificed to political influence or expediency. It matters little in its defection, whether the church dominates the state, or whether the state rules the church, the result in either case is an entangling alliance fatal to the spirituality and purity of the church in varying degrees. In both its ecclesiastical and political character Babylon has been guilty of the charge, "drunken with the blood of the saints," not simply in literal martyrdoms, but in the spiritual destruction of the souls of men. "The scarlet coloured beast" that carried the woman which afterward hated her, made her "desolate and naked" "and burnt her with fire," is typical of all ungodly alliances. Eventually they turn and rend each other according to the irony of fate in the bitterest antagonism—a just punishment of their iniquity.

The fall of Babylon is hinted in the fourth Cycle, Rev. 14:8, enlarged in the fifth, Rev. 16:19, and elaborately described in the sixth, Rev. 18:4-24. It matters not whether the basis of the figure was the destruction of ancient Babylon in Isa. 13:17-22, or the fall of Jerusalem predicted by Christ—a time of suffering unequalled hitherto in human history. It is taken as the type of the doom of the apostate church mentioned specifically six times: Rev. 14:8; 16:19; 17:5; 18:2; 18:10; 18:21. The entire 18th Chapter is a graphic description of her repudiation by Christ and her utter destruction at His Coming.

The Beast Re-appears

The first beast re-appears in this sixth Cycle as "scarlet-colored" and as carrying the woman, herself significantly "arrayed in purple and scarlet color"—two of a kind. There can be no mistaking his identity. The descriptions strictly correspond: "Full of the names of blasphemy, having seven heads and ten horns." Compare Rev. 13:1.

At his first appearance he is associated with the second beast as his ally. In the next Cycle he appears in company with "the false prophet"—another name for his same confederate. Now he re-appears the third time as the support and paramour of the harlot "arrayed in purple and scarlet." He appears always in the same role, whether "beast" or "kings," the personification of world powers and principles, the implacable foe of Christ and the saints. Of these "kings," his representatives, it is said: "These shall make war with the Lamb, and the Lamb shall overcome them; for he is Lord of Lords and King of Kings." This is in anticipation of the final defeat, described later, in the conflict with the King at his Second Coming leading His victorious hosts.

The Interlude

The Interlude with its songs of Consolation occurs just before the Second Coming and the overwhelming defeat of the ungodly forces at Armageddon, and consists of four "Alleluias:"

1. "I heard a great voice of much people in heaven saying:

> Alleluia; Salvation and glory and honor and power
> Unto the Lord our God:
> For true and righteous are his judgments;
> For he hath judged the great whore
> Which did corrupt the earth with her fornication.
> And hath avenged the blood of his servants at her hand.
> And again they said, Alleluia."

2. "And the four and twenty elders and the four beasts fell down and worshipped God that sat on the throne, saying: Amen. Alleluia."

3. Solo: "And a voice came out of the throne saying: Praise our God, all ye his servants, and ye that fear him, both small and great."

4. "And I heard as it were the voice of a great multitude, and as the voice of many waters and as the voice of mighty thunderings, saying:

> Alleluia; for the Lord God Omnipotent reigneth.
> Let us be glad and give honor to him;
> For the marriage of the Lamb is come
> And his wife hath made herself ready.
> And to her was granted that she should be arrayed
> In fine linen, clean and white:
> For the fine linen is the righteousness of the saints."

In striking contrast with the Kings of the earth lamenting the judgment upon the harlot, heaven is heard rejoicing over her saying: "Rejoice over her, thou heaven, and ye holy apostles and prophets; for God hath avenged you on her. . . . Blessed are they which are called to the marriage supper of the Lamb."

The Consummation and Second Coming

The cataclysm is at hand. The voice of the angel is about to sound the doom of time. The victorious King on a white horse accompanied by the armies of heaven leads his last campaign against evil. Armageddon is about to clear the way for the complete overthrow of the satanic allies and their utter annihilation.

Amid all these convulsions of nature and nations, the saints are absolutely secure. The chorus sings in advance the peans of victory: "Alleluia: for the Lord God Omnipotent reigneth" —not only in the spiritual realm, but throughout the vast universe of God.

Each time that the end of the Dispensation is shown in the various panoramas, the revelation becomes clearer reaching toward the climax. In the first Cycle, Christ is "standing at the door." Next His voice is heard: "Behold I come as a thief"—unexpectedly. Then appears "a white cloud and upon the cloud sits one like unto the Son of man, having on his head a golden crown and in his hand a sharp sickle." Now at length occurs an elaborate description of His triumphant march to victory:

"And I saw heaven opened, and behold a white horse; and he that sat upon him was called Faithful and True, and in righteousness he doth judge and make war. His eyes were as a flame of fire, and on his head were many crowns; and he had a name written, that no man knew, but he himself. And he was clothed with a vesture dipped in blood: and his name is called The Word of God.

"And the armies which were in heaven followed him upon white horses, clothed in fine linen, white and clean. And out of his mouth goeth a sharp sword, that with it he should smite the nations: and he shall rule them with a rod of iron;

and he treadeth the winepress of the fierceness and wrath of Almighty God. And he hath on his vesture and on his thigh a name written, KING OF KINGS, AND LORD OF LORDS."

The sixth Cycle of the Drama ends as in the previous with Armageddon and overwhelming victory:

"And I saw the beast, and the kings of the earth, and their armies, gathered together to make war against him that sat on the horse, and against his army. And the beast was taken, and with him the false prophet that wrought miracles before him, with which he deceived them that had received the mark of the beast, and them that worshipped his image. These both were cast alive into a lake of fire burning with brimstone."

The beast, symbolic of world forces and worldly principles, and the false prophet, typical of false faiths, are captured and cast into perdition. The completeness of the victory is emphasized in the statement: "The remnant were slain with the sword of him that sat upon the horse, which sword proceeded out of his mouth." "The remnant"—scattered fragments, leaderless and disorganized, utterly annihilated, not a unit left to rally for another opposition—what a striking expression of utter destruction!

Once more the curtain drops. It marks again the end of the Dispensation in the Drama of Christianity!

The SEVENTH CYCLE

TEXT: REVELATION XX

John: "And I saw an angel come down from heaven, having the key of the bottomless pit and a great chain in his hand. And he laid hold on the dragon, that old serpent, which is the Devil, and Satan, and bound him a thousand years, and cast him into the bottomless pit, and shut him up, and set a seal upon him, that he should deceive the nations no more, till the thousand years should be fulfilled: and after that he must be loosed a little season.

"And I saw thrones, and they sat upon them, and judgment was given unto them; and I saw the souls of them that were beheaded for the witness of Jesus, and for the word of God, and which had not worshipped the beast, neither his image, neither had received his mark upon their foreheads, or in their hands; and they lived and reigned with Christ a thousand years. But the rest of the dead lived not again until the thousand years were finished. This is the first resurrection.

"Blessed and holy is he that hath part in the first resurrection: on such the second death hath no power, but they shall be priests of God and of Christ, and shall reign with him a thousand years. And when the thousand years are expired, Satan shall be loosed out of his prison, and shall go out to deceive the nations which are in the four quarters of the earth, Gog and Magog, to gather them together to battle: the number of whom is as the sand of the sea.

"And they went up on the breadth of the earth, and compassed the camp of the saints about, and the beloved city: and fire came down from God out of heaven, and devoured them. And the devil that deceived them was cast into the lake of fire and brimstone, where the beast and the false prophet are, and shall be tormented day and night for ever and ever.

"And I saw a great white throne, and him that sat on it, from whose face the earth and the heaven fled away; and there was found no place for them.

"And I saw the dead, small and great stand before God; and the books were opened which is the book of life: and the dead were judged out of those things which were written in the books, according to their works.

"And the sea gave up the dead which were in it; and death and hell delivered up the dead which were in them: and they were judged every man according to their works.

"And death and hell were cast into the lake of fire. This is the second death. And whosoever was not found written in the book of life was cast into the lake of fire."

CHAPTER IX

The SUBJUGATION *and* DOOM *of* SATAN

THE Christian Dispensation from the Incarnation to the Second Coming of Christ is presented for the seventh and last time in the twentieth chapter of Revelation. The events therein narrated are not subsequent to the Second Coming as ordinarily assigned in the time-schedule of historic and various other interpreters, but coincide strictly with the period covered by the other panoramas. It presents an entirely new phase of the subject in the Drama of Christianity. Its specific purpose is to feature Satan's subjugation and more especially his final judgment.

The last Cycle related the fall of Babylon, the doom of the beast and of the false prophet. The judgment of Satan might well have been recorded as taking place in the same connection, as all of these events coincide in time; but instead one entire panorama—and appropriately the last—is devoted to the career and doom of Satan. It begins with his first conflict with Christ, covers his whole relation to the Christian Dispensation, his subjection to Christ during the entire period and ends with his complete overthrow and final doom. In accordance with the structural form and uniform method of presentation—which exhibits outstanding events, first as vague hints that are afterwards elaborately described in future panoramas—the doom of Satan is seen faintly like a dim flash of lightning in one vision that breaks in the subsequent as a lurid and terrific storm.

The Question of Interpretation

This twentieth chapter of the Apocalypse is confessedly one of the most difficult and disputed in the entire Word of God. It consists of four scenes in the Drama: 1—The Binding of Satan. 2—The Reign of the Martyrs. 3—Armageddon, the final Conflict between Satanic Hosts and the Saints. 4—The Resurrection, General Judgment and Doom of Satan. The first two are synchronous. The last two are intimately connected, following each other in quick succession.

The interpretation must be in strict accordance with the context, the structural plan and general purpose of the book. If the events described were contained in the historic or discursive portions of Scripture, the literal interpretation might be plausible, with a reasonable plea in favor of its acceptance. The distinctive characteristic of Apocalyptic literature is its uniform presentation of truth in symbolic form rather than in ordinary narrative. The literal rendering of figures and forms in Apocalyptic literature violates all the canons of interpretation and introduces confusion of thought in the effort to understand the mind of the Spirit. The truth can be best ascertained by approaching the subject unprejudiced and with no preconceived theory to sustain, but studied in the light of the Apocalyptic character of the book and the concurrent teaching of the whole tenor of Scripture.

1—*The Binding of Satan*

"And I saw an angel come down from heaven having the key of the bottomless pit and a great chain in his hand. And he laid hold on the dragon, that old serpent which is the Devil, and Satan, and bound him a thousand years. And cast him into the bottomless pit, and shut him up, and set a seal upon him, that he should deceive the nations no more, till the thousand years should be fulfilled: and after that he must be loosed a little season."

Is this language to be interpreted literally? If so, it is the one exception in the whole symbolic book. In his famous address Patrick Henry asks at the beginning of the American Revolution, "Shall we lie supinely on our backs till our enemies have bound us hand and foot?" Does any one understand that "binding" except in a figurative sense? Did "the angel" have a literal "chain?" Could a spirit be bound with such? Can this language, fairly interpreted, and in the light of other Scripture, mean anything else than the limitation of his power and the suspension of his malicious activity?

In its essential features are not the "casting out" of Satan in chapter twelve and this "binding" in chapter twenty practically identical, the difference being a change of the figure of speech and the latter account a fuller development of the previous statement of the same event? The parallel undoubtedly is remarkably striking.

If "Scripture is the interpreter of Scripture," confirmation of this contention may confidently be sought in the appeal to other portions of the revealed Word. Is there any one better able to interpret the binding of Satan than Christ himself? Is not His parable of "the binding of the strong man," Matt. 12:29, a disguised allusion to His future subjugation of the common adversary of God and the saints? Other hints of the same event abound in His instruction of the disciples. "I saw Satan as lightning fall from heaven," can have no other significance than his overthrow as more fully related in the Apocalypse. In His prophetic allusion to His approaching cross, He distinctly connects the judgment of Satan with that event in His own life: "Now shall the prince of this world be cast out. And I if I be lifted up, will draw all men unto me." In His last discourse He proclaims as if it were already an accomplished fact: "The prince of this world *hath been judged.*" Paul, with keener insight and fuller comprehension of the significance of the cross than the combined apostolic college, alludes to it as the means by which Christ had "spoiled principalities and powers," and "made a show of them openly, triumphing over them in it"—the subjugation of Satan and his spiritual forces. Do not these statements corroborate the truth of this interpretation, not only confirming the identity and the casting out and binding of Satan, but distinctly indicating the cross as the means of Satan's conquest?

With all of his satanic shrewdness it can scarcely be supposed that he had foreknowledge of the future and thorough acquaintance with the plans and purposes of God. In the initial progress of his rebellion he probably did not know of the certainty and consequences of his utter defeat, nor of the method by which it would be ultimately accomplished. Still struggling for supremacy and planning to thwart the divine purpose, he overreached himself in bringing about the crucifixion. Not until the actual event took place did he realize that the cross was the means of the complete triumph of Christ in the work of redemption and the absolute conquest of himself, resulting in the utter failure of all his hopes and malicious planning. It was the signal for his casting out of heaven, and the limitation of his authority and activity by his ignominious binding. With what bitter chagrin and gnashing of teeth must he have heard the celebration of the event in heaven as it was heralded by "a loud voice, saying: Now is come Salvation, and Strength and the Kingdom of our God and the power of his Christ: for the accuser of our brethren is cast down, which accused them before our God day and night!" Is not this a sufficient explanation of his impotent rage—"having great wrath, because he knoweth that he hath but a short time." Does not this illuminate the statement of Christ: "The prince of this world hath been judged." Sentence being pronounced upon the arch criminal of the universe, he learns doubtless for the first time that his career is practically ended. The execution of the sentence begins with his binding; and the "short time" of respite coincides with the Christian Dispensation, likely to terminate at any moment by the imminent return of the Lord of heaven and earth for the utter annihilation of the satanic allies at Armageddon and the casting of himself "into the lake of fire and brimstone," to be "tormented day and night forever and ever."

The Extent and Limitation of His Binding

It may be objected by some that this interpretation is inconsistent with statements warning believers against the machinations and activity of Satan. "Resist the devil," said

James; and amplified by Peter is the warning: "Your adversary the devil as a roaring lion, walketh about seeking whom he may devour."

Prof. Milligan interprets the binding and loosing as synchronous, each covering the entire Christian Dispensation, explaining that while Satan was completely conquered and bound by Christ, he was immediately "loosed for a little season," signifying partial liberty in fulfilment of the purpose of God—just as others explain his loosing near the end of the Dispensation. It is, however, an interpretation purely personal and private, which can neither be substantiated nor disproved.

Utterly regardless of the various and varying interpretations of the binding of Satan, it is universally agreed that he is most effectually bound and impotent to injure one of God's children, each being as safe as if Satan were literally as well as absolutely "bound with a great chain." Warnings to "resist the devil" fall into the same category as exhortations to perseverance notwithstanding the repeated assurances of the absolute safety of believers in such promises as are given by Christ and reiterated by Paul: "And I give unto them eternal life; and they shall never perish, neither shall any man pluck them out of my hand." "For I am persuaded that neither death, nor life, nor angels, nor principalities, nor powers, nor things present, nor things to come, nor height, nor depth, nor any other creature, shall be able to separate us from the love of God which is in Christ Jesus our Lord." No matter what power or influence he may exert over others, the children of God are absolutely safe. They have been redeemed with the blood of Christ. They are one with Him. His life is their life. They are as safe as if they were already on the throne with Him and their adversary already "cast into the lake of fire and brimstone."

No matter what interpretation may be placed upon the binding of Satan, his emissaries and agents are not bound, and in resisting them believers are resisting the devil himself, being assured that "we wrestle not against flesh and blood, but against principalities, against powers, against the rulers of the darkness of this world, against spiritual wickedness in high places," and need "the whole armor of God" in this militant age of the church.

It may be still further objected that he was no longer to "deceive the nations," while as a matter of fact the nations are still characterized by ungodly ambitions and cursed by the ravages of war and other devices of the devil. To this a two-fold answer might appropriately be given:

(1)—Nowhere in the account of the binding of Satan is there promised an era of universal righteousness. This is a gratuitous assumption read into the narrative. The object of this twentieth chapter is to prophesy the complete subjugation of Satan and not to promise a long period of prosperity and blessedness—a golden age of uninterrupted peace. The popular conception of the Millennium as an era of universal righteousness has led the church far afield, being utterly contrary to the teaching of Christ who seriously questioned whether upon His return he would even "find faith on the earth." It is equally inconsistent with the whole tenor and teaching of the Apocalypse, whose consistent purpose in every part and panorama is to forewarn of the martyr-spirit which is to characterize the life of the church to the very end of the Dispensation.

(2)—It may be also very pertinently and forcefully urged that nowhere is it said, or even implied, that the beast and the false prophet are bound; and ungodly human nature is not changed. Otherwise there would have been no need of the Great Commission to evangelize the world.

"The New Testament in Modern Speech," the joint product of Richard Francis Weymouth and his scholarly editor, commenting on this text, suggests the binding of Satan at the beginning of the Christian Era, and that "the devil's work of tempting and injuring mankind has had to be done for him with inferior power and skill and diminished success by subordinate evil spirits." If their presence and pernicious activity be recognized in addition to the beast and the false prophet and depraved human nature, surely this would be sufficient force and agency to account for the present ungodly state of the world without any need of Satan's personal presence and activity.

This interpretation of the binding of Satan is consistent with the teaching of Christ, the general tenor of Scripture and all the facts in the case, equivalent in this symbolic book to the limitation of Satan's power and activity—the first victory of Christ and His cross.

The Significance of the Thousand Years

If this number is to be taken literally, it is the solitary instance in this unique book abounding in mystic characters and symbolic numbers. Does anyone interpret its numerous "sevens" literally, or the "six hundred three score and six," the "one hundred and forty and four thousand," the "forty and two months" or "the three and a half years"? Just as "seven" is the symbol of perfection, so "the thousand years" is the symbol of a long indefinite period of time, so used elsewhere in Scripture and in ordinary speech. "For a thousand years in thy sight is but as yesterday when it is passed, and as a watch in the night."—Psalm 90:4. "One day is with the Lord as a thousand years and a thousand years as one day."—II Peter, 3:8. Does anyone interpret either one of these literally, as signifying an exact period of time? How can there be the slightest possibility, therefore, of misunderstanding the significance of the phrase "a thousand years" in this case?

Six times in this twentieth chapter occurs the same expression "a thousand years." Is there any reason for not interpreting it in accordance with its usage elsewhere in Scripture as suggestive of a long indefinite period? In that case it would appropriately represent the entire period of the Christian Dispensation, indefinite in the number of the years but very definite as to the exact period covered. The Post and Pre-millennialists are unquestionably alike wrong in their literal interpretation. The thousand years is the symbol of a long indefinite period commensurate with the Christian Dispensation, necessarily uncertain by reason of the imminence of the Second Coming, which will *ipso facto* terminate the period.

The phrase is commonly used in the same sense in ordinary speech. During the writing of this treatise its author heard one say, "I have made this statement a thousand times." Did he understand the speaker literally; or as a common expression conveying the idea of a large indefinite number of times? The Scriptures themselves employ language in the common usage and speak of the sun rising and setting. The "thousand years" is, therefore, the adaptation of language in its common usage to convey the thought of a period of years, coinciding with the militant age of the church rather than an era of universal righteousness—gratuitously supplied but conspicuously lacking in the narrative.

The Reign of the Saints

"And I saw thrones, and they sat upon them, and judgment was given unto them; and I saw the souls of them that were beheaded for the witness of Jesus, and for the word of God, and which had not worshipped the beast, neither his image, neither had received his mark upon their foreheads, or in their hands; and they lived and reigned with Christ a thousand years."

In his vision John saw (1)—"the souls" of the martyrs—disembodied spirits. (2)—"Thrones and they sat upon them." The crucial test of the interpretation is the question, Where were these thrones located. Dr. Eugene C. Caldwell, Professor of New Testament Interpretation in Union Theological Seminary, Richmond, Va., in his scholarly pamphlet entitled, "The Millennium," directs attention to the fact that this expression "throne" occurs forty-five times in the Apocalypse, and with the exception of the two references to Satan's seat and the throne of the beast, Rev. 2:13; 16:10, the "thrones" are always located in heaven—unless this is a solitary exception. Of the forty-three "throne" texts, unquestionably forty-two refer to a throne in heaven. If the thrones of the martyrs are upon earth rather than in heaven, the burden of proof must be furnished by the advocates of that supposition. Is this one disputed text sufficient to teach an earthly reign of saints?

Appealing again to the parallelism of the structural form of the Apocalypse, by which the same events and scenes reappear in the various panoramas, attention is directed to the close parallel between Rev. 7:14-17 and this reign of the saints in Rev. 20:4. In the first case they "came out of great tribulation;" in the second, they "were beheaded for the witness of Jesus." Are they the same parties? The first reference unquestionably locates them in heaven. If they are not the same, is there any reason to infer that the first are in heaven, and the second class are on earth?

The difficulties of an earthly reign are insuperable. 1—Is this reign to be a mixture of living peoples and "souls" of the sainted dead? 2—Will they reign as disembodied spirits over souls in mortal bodies? 3—Will they be in glorified bodies mingling with souls in corruptible bodies? 4—Why should Satan be turned loose upon such an ideal state of affairs, converting a heaven on earth into a veritable hell? Unless there can be given some satisfactory explanation, or at least plausible, these questions must raise a doubt in the minds of thoughtful students of God's Word as to the reasonableness of this supposed earthly reign of martyred saints. The text itself contains not the slightest suggestion of such; and we have no warrant for asking acceptance of any theory, which is not strongly supported by scriptural authority. The conclusion is overwhelmingly against any supposed earthly reign of the saints.

The Two Resurrections

Once again necessity compels the inquiry, Is this language in a highly symbolical book intended to be understood in a strictly literal sense? Great fundamental principles and far-reaching programs, affecting the future interests of the kingdom and the glorified estate of the saints, are not elsewhere based upon a single obscure passage of Scripture. The theory of two resurrections inferred from this text is doubtfully sustained by its advocates in an appeal to certain passages of Scripture containing the Greek preposition "ek," which may be rendered "out from among," such as Paul's expressed hope in Phil. 3:11, of being able to "attain unto the resurrection of the dead." By so translating the preposition "ek" in such texts, we have the rendering "resurrection out from among the dead," by which it is argued that Paul's implied desire was to be accounted worthy of being found in a privileged class, honored by being raised from the dead in advance of the general resurrection.

It must be admitted that in all such interpretations involving the unknown future, dogmatism is out of place. Sincerity of purpose and loyalty to theories of supposed scriptural basis are not in themselves sufficient proofs of the infallibility of exegesis and correctness of interpretation. Arguments are hereby submitted in favor of a more reasonable interpretation, based chiefly on corroborative scriptural statements.

1—*The Argument From Analogy*

The mind of the church, overwhelmingly prevalent throughout the ages, understands the two resurrections as: 1—Spiritual, equivalent to Regeneration. 2—The General Resurrection of the body, both of the righteous and the wicked simultaneously. The Scripture confessedly teaches that as the result of sin the penalty is death of two kinds: 1—Spiritual, the penalty inflicted on Adam immediately in fulfilment of the threat, "In the day thou eatest thereof thou shall surely die," and inherited by all his posterity, involving later the death of the body. 2—"The Second Death," visited upon the impenitent wicked, involving the literal death of both soul and body.

Reasoning from analogy the first death being spiritual would correspond to a "first resurrection" which is also spiritual. The "second death" being literal would correspond to a second and literal resurrection of the body in order that it may literally participate either in the reward of the glorified in eternal life, or share the penalty of the wicked in "a second death." Does not this shed a flood of light on the statement of the context, "Blessed and holy is he that hath part in the first resurrection: on such the second death hath no power."

2—*The Scriptural Argument*

Regeneration undoubtedly is sometimes described as a spiritual resurrection, as for example in such texts as Eph. 2:1 "And you hath he *quickened*—supplied from the context—who were dead in trespasses and sins;" Col. 2:13. "And you, being *dead* in your sons and the uncircumcision of your flesh, hath he *quickened,* together with him;" and Rom. 6:4. "As Christ was raised up from the dead by the glory of the Father, even so we also should walk in newness of life"—as the result of a spiritual resurrection.

Christ, the supreme authority, in His prophetic office as teacher, seems to contrast the spiritual and bodily resurrection, recorded by the author of the Apocalypse, in his Gospel, John 5:25-29: "Verily, verily, I say unto you, the hour is coming, *and now is,* when the dead shall hear the voice of the Son of God; and they that hear shall live." This was used by Christ *in the present tense*—unquestionably a spiritual resurrection. Notice the striking contrast in the same connection: "Marvel not at this; for *the hour is coming* in the which all that are *in the graves* shall hear his voice and shall come forth; they that have done good, unto the resurrection of life; and they that have done evil, unto the resurrection of damnation." This latter statement involves three things: 1—The event is future—*"The hour is coming."* 2—The parties are *"in the grave."* 3—The resurrection of those "that have done good" and those "that have done evil" impliedly is simultaneous. The two resurrections recorded by John in his Gospel and the two resurrections recorded by John in his Apocalypse are evidently identical.

On one other occasion Christ makes a distinction between the spiritually dead and the literally dead, saying, "Let the dead bury their dead," Luke 9:60. If further confirmation is needed to determine the time of the resurrection of the righteous ,appeal may be made still further to the authority of Christ who twice asserts that believers will be "raised up at the last day." See John 6:39-40.

The Loosing of Satan

"And when the thousand years are expired, Satan shall be loosed out of his prison, and shall go out to deceive the nations which are in the four quarters of the earth, Gog and Magog, to gather them together to battle; the number of whom is as the sand of the sea."

The expiration of "the thousand years" and the loosing of Satan for "a little season," may serve as the appropriate place and occasion to consider the merits of opposing interpretations, leading to the conviction as to the truth of the Millennial theory. The mistake of the Postmillennialist is in looking for a Millennium rather than for the Second Coming of Christ. He reads into the binding of Satan for "a thousand years" a golden age through the preaching of the Gospel, which must precede the Second Coming. This is utterly inconsistent with the imminence of His coming, taught by Christ and the Apostles. Its pending is always a fact. Its possibility is always "at hand." The fact that it has been delayed for nearly two thousand years does not in the slightest alter its imminence. Death is an event always imminent, notwithstanding the fact that health and physical constitution may postpone the event in some cases a hundred years; but these do not militate against its immediate possibility at any time. A world of accidents and the contingency of disease may cause death any moment—always imminent no matter how long delayed.

The Second Coming of Christ may be known to the Father as a delayed event, but that does not affect the contingency of its possibility and pendency. If, however, "a thousand years" must necessarily intervene beforehand, that would unquestionably affect its contingent imminence. Looking backward in this twentieth century we can place an interpretation on "the thousand years," which would not have been justified beforehand. At no age of the church's history has it authority to teach that much time must necessarily elapse before the Coming can take place.

Clear distinction must be made between His "Coming in His kingdom," and His Coming in person. They are in no sense the same thing. In the Yellowstone Park the geyser known as "Old Faithful" is gathering its steam and filling its basin every moment for the approaching eruption, which takes place suddenly as the inevitable result. "Coming in His kingdom" is a progressive event always taking place and promised to certain parties as something to be witnessed before they should "taste of death."—Matt. 16:28. The prayer, "Thy kingdom come," has reference primarily to the first contingency but preparing the way—as in the eruption of Old Faithful—for the lightning-like flash of the Second Coming in person. The latter is sure, inevitable, imminent, but may, by certain influences and causes, be indefinitely delayed. The Coming of Christ employed in Scripture in a double sense may be viewed as one event, the "Coming in His Kingdom" issuing eventually in His Coming in person.

The theory of the Premillennialist, on the other hand, is at fault in adopting a man-made "program" for Christ, based upon an interpretation of Scripture which fits a certain idea of the kingdom. The schedule of this program is substantially as follows: 1—The appearance of Christ in the air. 2—The Rapture of the Church. 3—The Tribulation of the World. 4—The Second Coming—in reality a third Coming. 5—The Millennial Reign. 6—The Loosing of Satan and Armageddon. 7—The Resurrection of the Wicked and General Judgment.

Premillennialists follow each other in this program as if it were inspired, and some are so dogmatic that if any are so presumptuous as to differ from their view it is equivalent to rejecting the Word of God. It must be admitted that it cannot be dogmatically disproved. It may be true; but it is based upon a mixture of literal and fanciful interpretations, regarded by many as a well nigh infallible revelation of the mind of the Spirit. It has been adopted by many of the most earnest and consecrated children of God, who long for a return of their dear Lord with a passion worthy of the highest commendation; but it does not commend itself, nor carry conviction, to the vast multitude of Christian people as saintly, as scholarly, as loyal to the Word of God, and who pray as fervently, "Come Lord Jesus, come quickly." It has influenced some of the more extreme to fix the time by "calculations" and by "the signs of the times"—although Christ Himself discouraged such, by asserting the impossibility of such forecasting, saying: "But of that day and that hour knoweth no man, no, not the angels which are in heaven, neither the Son, but the Father."—Mark 13:32.

The Church Age vs. The Kingdom

The distinction between the *present* church-age and the *future* kingdom-age is not scriptural; neither is the distinction between "the kingdom of God" and "the kingdom of heaven." On the contrary the latter are used interchangeably by Christ and the Apostles. One inspired Evangelist quotes Jesus as saying, "The kingdom of heaven is like unto leaven."—Matt. 13:33; and another records Him as saying, "The kingdom of God" is like leaven.—Luke 13:21. The labored effort to void the conclusion that the two are interchangeable has failed to satisfy thoughtful students of the Word of God.

The kingdom does not coincide strictly with "the visible church," for Christ says it "cometh not with observation," but the visible church does come "with observation." The kingdom does not correspond strictly with "the invisible church," for it is partly in heaven and partly on earth, and does not contain both "good" and "bad," as does the kingdom of heaven.—Matt. 13:47-49.

The best definition perhaps which can be given is: The kingdom of God is Christ's spiritual rule in the hearts of men. Its nearest synonym is Christianity. Apply it to Christ's parables of the kingdom and see how nearly they correspond. Christianity "is like unto a grain of mustard seed . . . which indeed is the least of all seeds; but when it is grown it is the greatest among herbs"—illustrating its insignificant beginning and its marvelous outward development. Christianity "is like unto leaven"—in its internal transforming power. The objection is often raised that it cannot be true because of the subsequent statement, "till the whole was leavened"; and Christianity does not and is not supposed to convert the whole world. Yet the statement of its leavening influence is true nevertheless. Christianity has not converted the whole United States, but it can be truly stated that it has leavened the whole. Multitudes who have not been converted have nevertheless felt the leaven of its influence in accordance with the statement of Christ.

Christianity "is likened unto a man which sowed good seed in his field; but while men slept, his enemy came and sowed tares among the wheat." Whether the tares were false teaching or evil practices, there is no possibility of separating them till "the harvest, the end of the world." Some of these parables can apply only to true Christianity as "Seek ye first the kingdom of God and his righteousness": "The kingdom of God cometh not with observation": and "Thy kingdom come." According to the Apostle Paul, "The kingdom of God" is not an age or dispensation, "but righteousness and peace, and joy in the Holy Ghost."—Rom. 14:17.

From these considerations we are entitled to differ from our worthy Premillennial brethren in our maintenance that the kingdom of God is present and not wholly future. According to Christ the kingdom is "within you"—or "among you," if that rendering is preferred. It is spiritual, progressive, visible, invisible and everlasting—not terminated by the loosing of Satan "for a little season."

John Calvin rejected the Millennial reign of Christ. See Institutes, Vol. II, Book III, Chapter 25. Augustine identified the Millennium with the militant age of the church, just as this study does. The Westminster Confession of Faith enthrones Christ as "executing the office of king, in subduing us unto Himself, in ruling and defending us, and in restraining all His and our enemies."

Dr. R. C. Reed, late professor of Ecclesiastical History and Church Polity in Columbia Theological Seminary, in his last Treatise, "What is the Kingdom of God," argues forcefully for the present reign and spiritual lordship of Christ:

"Christ is now a King, executing royal functions, not merely an heir apparent. His sway is not confined to the church, but extends to all His enemies, whether men or devils. Some persons think that the devil is exercising supreme and independent control over this world during the present dispensation. But that at the second advent, Christ will bind him in the bottomless pit. The more rational and scriptural view is that he is now under the restraint symbolized by the binding with a chain. We recall how that the demons could not enter the herd of swine, could not even hurt a hog without permission of Jesus. Christ is 'head over all things to the church, which in His body, the fulness of Him that filleth all things.' 'All power in heaven and earth is given into His hands.' If this does not constitute Kingship, what does? Must we see the King with the crown and sceptre and body guard and army? Are we so wedded to material and sensuous things that we can see no glory, no regal splendor in spiritual lordship?"

Misconceptions of Prophecy

The prophetic writings of the Old Testament, forecasting the glorious kingdom of righteousness under the peaceful reign of Christ, have been singularly misapprehended and misapplied. It has been said that oftentimes "prophecies must be read backward," before we can be absolutely sure of the correct apprehension of their true significance. History has compelled many reversals of judgment in the interpretations of prophetic writings.

1—The Jews interpreted the prophecies of the Messiah and His glorious reign literally and as synchronous with the First Coming of Christ. They anticipated an earthly kingdom of power and splendor, which would annihilate the Roman Empire and establish a Jewish kingdom in its stead at Jerusalem, rivaling the glory and pomp of Solomon's reign, extending its sway over all the nations of earth. Their false conception of the mission of their expected Messiah caused His rejection by the nation. "He came unto His own, and His own received Him not," because He did not conform unto their type but instead proposed a spiritual kingdom of personal righteousness.

2—The Postmillennialists have interpreted the prophecies as forecasting a Millennium, ushering in a golden age of the triumph of Christianity, notwithstanding the fact that the Scriptures forewarn "a falling away"—the Dispensation ending in disaster, and Christ Himself raising the inquiry whether at His Coming He shall even "find faith on the earth."

3—The Premillennialists interpret these prophecies as literally as did the Jews, except that they apply them to the Second Coming, but setting up just such a temporal kingdom as was anticipated by the Jews. Even the very Jewish sacrifices are to be restored in the Millennium. It is to be a kingdom ruled by the sword—a type repudiated by Christ. It is to be a mixture of supernatural beings—"souls"—ruling men in the flesh, a mixture of good and evil, interrupted by a terrific revolt against Christ and the enthroned saints, led by Satan, turned loose on this peaceful world while enjoying the blessedness of the personal reign of Christ.

Are not all the parties equally at fault in applying the prophecies? May not these prophecies have a dual significance, having first a spiritual fulfilment in the present Messianic reign of Christ on His mediatorial throne, and in the hearts of men, and their final and full realization in the future glorious kingdom—"everlasting"—uninterrupted by any revolt, Satan and his evil forces being forever eliminated? Does not Messianic prophecy find its final fulfilment in "the New Jerusalem coming down from God out of heaven"—creating "a new heavens and a new earth wherein dwelleth righteousness?" Is not this the significance of the magnificent closing prophecy of Isaiah—almost the identical language of Peter and of the Apocalypse—thereby confirming this interpretation: "For as the new heavens and the new earth, which I will make, shall remain before me, saith the Lord, so shall your seed and your name remain, and . . . all flesh shall come to worship before me, saith the Lord."—Isaiah 66:22-23.

Reconciliation of Views

May not Post- and Pre-millennialists, who have so much in common, agree upon the following irreducible minimum as the expression of the blessed hope of both, and of the church itself? 1—The Second Coming of Christ is both personal and imminent. "Behold he cometh with the clouds and every eye shall see him."—Rev. 1:7. "This same Jesus, which is taken up from you into heaven, shall so come *in like manner* as ye have seen him go into heaven."—Acts 1:11. "Behold, I come quickly."—Rev. 3:11; 22:12; 22:20.

2—The Second Coming ends the Christian Dispensation. "And they shall see the Son of man coming in the clouds of heaven with power and great glory, and he shall send his angels with a great sound of a trumpet, and they shall gather together his elect from the four winds, from one end of heaven unto the other."—Matt. 24:30-31. "The harvest is the end of the world; and the reapers are the angels."—Matt. 13:39.

3—The Second Coming introduces the visible reign of Christ and the saints, whether millennial or eternal. Why not leave that as an open question? The blessed hope is the return of our Lord, and not the Millennium. There is no fundamental difference as to the faith of all parties in the ultimate triumph of Christ, and the church and their joint reign, whether millennial or eternal. Instead of controversy and recriminations, why not agree to join together in the common prayer, "Come, Lord Jesus, come quickly."

Armageddon and the Doom of Satan

Each time the Dispensation ends it features a new phase of the Drama. In this case, Armageddon previously mentioned, and by name for the first time, in the fifth Cycle, Rev. 16:16, described somewhat at length in the sixth, Rev. 19:17-20, is now at length given its deserved prominence as marking the complete subjugation of Satan, and as sharing the fate of the beast and false prophet—the reward of his blasphemous iniquity as the author of sin and suffering in the universe of God.

"And they went up on the breadth of the earth and compassed the camp of the saints about, and the beloved city; and fire came down from God out of heaven and devoured them. And the devil that deceived them was cast into the lake of fire and brimstone, where the beast and the false prophet are, and shall be tormented day and night forever and ever.

"And I saw a great white throne, and him that sat on it, from whose face the earth and the heaven fled away; and there was found no place for them. And I saw the dead, small and great, stand before God; and the books were opened, which is the book of life: and the dead were judged out of those things which were written in the books, according to their works.

"And the sea gave up the dead which were in it; and death and hell delivered up the dead which were in them; and they were judged every man according to their works."

At the close of the Dispensation in each panorama the Second Coming is prominently featured, but in this last Cycle it seems conspicuously lacking in the judgment of some. Such, however, is not the case, as may be judged from the following striking presentation of evidence by Dr. Eugene C. Caldwell in his pamphlet on the Millennium:

"The coming down of fire out of heaven and devouring Satan and his hosts may be an apocalyptic symbol for the Second Coming of Christ to rescue and reward his people and destroy his and their enemies.

"'And they compassed the camp of the saints about and the beloved city; and fire came down out of heaven and devoured them.' Fire in Scripture is often the symbol of God, and here it evidently denotes some signal divine intervention just before the general resurrection and final judgment, when the saints are represented as in desperate need of superhuman aid. Paul in 2 Thess. 1:4-10, 1 Cor. 3:10-15, and Peter in 2 Pet. 3:10, picture the Second Coming under the symbol of fire. 'We ourselves glory in you in the churches of God for your steadfastness and faith in all your persecutions and afflictions; to the end that ye may be counted worthy of the kingdom of God, if so be that it is a righteous thing with God to recompense affliction to them that afflict you, and to you that are afflicted rest with us, at the revelation (apocalypse) of the Lord Jesus from heaven with the angels of his power *in flaming fire,* rendering vengeance to them that know not God and obey not the Gospel of our Lord Jesus, who shall suffer eternal destruction from the face of the Lord and the glory of his power when he shall come to be glorified in his saints . . . in that day."—2 Thess. 1:4-10.

"Hence to interpret the descent of fire in Revelation 20:9 as an apocalyptic symbol to the Second Advent is in perfect accord with the uniform teaching of the New Testament and also in beautiful harmony with the organic structure of the book of Revelation as a whole. In immediate connection with the descent of fire (20:9), we have a description of the Second Coming in vs. 11: 'And I saw a great white throne and him that sat upon it, from whose face the earth and the heaven fled away.' Christ comes on a great white throne before which heaven and earth and all things flee away. In 14:14 Christ is pictured as coming on a white cloud, in 19:11 as coming on a white horse, and here the Second Advent is depicted as the appearance of Messiah seated on a white throne.

"Each one of the five panoramas—the seven seals, the seven trumpets, the seven symbolic figures, the seven bowls, and the sevenfold judgment—carries us to the Second Coming. And if chapter 20 with the thousand year period is, as we claim, a complete panorama in itself parallel with the others, then we would expect that it too would close with the Second Coming. And so it does, as symbolized in the descent of fire from heaven overwhelming the wicked and ushering in the Second Advent, the general resurrection and final judgment.

"It is of vital importance to note that Christ will return only at the close and culmination of the period of the church militant. Because of the presence and power of her Lord in her in the person of the Holy Spirit, the church advances through the deeps of time conquering and to conquer, ever gaining increasing victory; and on the eve of the final battle against sin her Lord will appear in person and himself lead her into the last charge and share with her the fruits of the victory."

The Resurrection and General Judgment

The great rebellion is crushed forever with the subjugation and doom of Satan. Nothing remains but the final scene of the Drama, the judgment of the dead. In a previous panorama this awful scene is reached at its close. It is specifically mentioned "and thy wrath is come and the time of the dead that they should be judged and that thou shouldst give reward unto thy servants," etc.—Rev. 11:18.

This brief hint is now expanded in this, the last panorama, giving a realistic and graphic account of the scene, exhibiting the great white throne, the opening of the books and the judgment of the dead. The final separation between good and evil is staged; and "death and hell cast into the lake of fire."

The Drama of Christianity is enacted for the seventh and last time. The curtain drops. Beyond is Eternity!

The EPILOGUE

TEXT: REV. XXI-XXII

John: "And I saw a new heaven and a new earth; for the first heaven and the first earth were passed away; and there was no more sea. And I John saw the holy city, new Jerusalem, coming down from God out of heaven, prepared as a bride adorned for her husband. And I heard a great voice out of heaven saying,

Heavenly Voice: "Behold, the tabernacle of God is with men, and he will dwell with them, and they shall be his people and God himself shall be with them, and be their God. And God shall wipe away all tears from their eyes; and there shall be no more death, neither sorrow, nor crying, neither shall there be any more pain: for the former things are passed away."

King on Throne: "Behold, I make all things new. . . . I am Alpha and Omega, the beginning and the end. I will give unto him that is athirst of the fountain of the water of life freely. He that overcometh shall inherit all things; and I will be his God, and he shall be my son." . . .

John: "And there came unto me one of the seven angels which had the seven vials full of the seven last plagues, and talked with me, saying, Come hither, I will shew thee the bride, the Lamb's wife. And he carried me away in the spirit to a great and high mountain, and shewed me that great city, the holy Jerusalem, descending out of heaven from God, having the glory of God: and her light was like unto a stone most precious, even like a jasper stone, clear as crystal.

"And had a wall great and high, and had twelve gates, and at the gates twelve angels, and names written thereon, which are the names of the twelve tribes of the children of Israel: on the east three gates; on the north three gates; on the south three gates; and on the west three gates. And the wall of the city had twelve foundations, and in them the names of the twelve apostles of the Lamb. . . .

"And I saw no temple therein; for the Lord God Almighty and the Lamb are the temple of it. And the city had no need of the sun, neither of the moon to shine in it: for the glory of God did lighten it, and the Lamb is the light thereof.

"And the nations of them which are saved shall walk in the light of it: and the kings of the earth do bring their glory and honour into it. And the gates of it shall not be shut at all by day; for there shall be no night there. . . .

"And he shewed me a pure river of water of life, clear as crystal proceeding out of the throne of God and of the Lamb. In the midst of the street of it and on either side of the river, was there the tree of life which bare twelve manner of fruits, and yielded her fruit every month: and the leaves of the tree were for the healing of the nations.

"And there shall be no more curse; but the throne of God and of the Lamb shall be in it; and his servants shall serve him: and they shall see his face, and his name shall be in their foreheads. And there shall be no night there; and they need no candle, neither light of the sun; for the Lord God giveth them light: and they shall reign for ever and ever." . . .

Jesus: "Behold, I come quickly: blessed is he that keepeth the saying of the prophecy of this book. . . . He that is unjust, let him be unjust still: and he which is filthy, let him be filthy still: and he that is righteous let him be righteous still: and he that is holy, let him be holy still.

"And, behold, I come quickly; and my reward is with me, to give every man according as his work shall be. I am Alpha and Omega, the beginning and the end, theh first and the last. Blessed are they that do his commandments, that they may have right to the tree of life, and may enter in through the gates into the city. . . .

"I Jesus have sent mine angel to testify unto you these things in the churches. I am the root and the offspring of David, and the bright and morning star.

"And the spirit and the bride say, Come. And let him that heareth say, Come. And let him that is athirst come. And whosoever will, let him take the water of life freely." . . .

John: "He which testifieth these things saith, Surely I come quickly. Amen. Even so, come. Lord Jesus. The grace of our Lord Jesus Christ be with you all. Amen."

CHAPTER X

The NEW JERUSALEM

THE last Cycle contained no Interlude, because no consolation was longer needed, being the close of the Drama—unless the Epilogue, with its description of the new Jerusalem, constitutes such consolation as compensation for earth's trials. The meaning and purpose of the book were intended as assurance to the church in the fires of persecution that no matter how desperate its condition, no matter how strong and malignant its bitterest foes, no matter how fierce the opposition, nor how excruciating the anguish of its sufferings, the ultimate triumph of righteousness and of the Kingdom of God was as sure as the omnipotent power of God, the eternal promises and the supreme over-ruling divine providence could guarantee the absolute certainty of any future event.

Beyond the closing act of the Drama, there is exhibited in brief flashlight the dim vista of eternity: "And I saw a new heaven and a new earth, for the first heaven and the first earth were passed away, and there was no more sea"—the latter being the emblem of changing moods and unchanging restlessness. The mutable has forever passed. The eternal is now the established order of the universe.

It is the fulfilment of the prophecy of Peter and of Isaiah 65:22—the blessed hope alike of the Old and New Testament: "Nevertheless we, according to his promise, look for new heavens and a new earth wherein dwelleth righteousness"—2 Peter 3:13—sin and injustice eliminated, righteousness triumphant. This sustains the contention of the author in the last chapter, that the prophetic visions of the glory of the kingdom of Christ could not find their fulfilment in a brief millennium, interrupted by the loosing of Satan, introducing the most awful period in the history of the world. The "new heaven and new earth" of Rev. 21:1 is an inspired interpretation, identifying the fulfilment with the blessed era *beyond the day of Judgment.*

The New Creation

If further confirmation were needed, it is furnished by the identification of this era with the New Jerusalem:

"And I, John, saw the holy city, new Jerusalem, coming down from God out of heaven, prepared as a bride adorned for her husband. And I heard a great voice out of heaven saying, Behold, the tabernacle of God is with men, and he will dwell with them, and they shall be his people, and God himself shall be with them, and be their God. And God shall wipe away all tears from their eyes; and there shall be no more death, neither sorrow, nor crying, neither shall there by any more pain: for the former things are passed away. And he that sat upon the throne said, Behold, I make all things new. And he said unto me, Write: for these words are true and faithful."

The golden age of poet and of prophet is more glorious than either dreamed "in all their golden fancies." The glorious transformation of this sin-cursed earth, revealed in rapturous vision of Old Testament prophecy and in New Testament hopes, is something far beyond the anticipation of the most ardent millennialist, whether Post or Pre.

Instead of our earth being burnt up or destroyed, it is destined to pass through a purifying process, being "reserved unto fire against the day of judgment. . . . wherein the heavens being on fire shall be dissolved, and the elements shall melt with fervent heat." Just as it issued, however, from its baptism of water in the Noachian Deluge, so it will survive its baptism of fire as "a new earth wherein dwelleth righteousness."

The Home of the Redeemed

It is destined to be the eternal abode of the saints—not a heaven located far away in some distant world. If there had been no fall in Eden, this earth would undoubtedly have constituted the inheritance of unfallen humanity. Christ recovered for us what was lost in Adam. Consequently the Bible closes with Paradise Regained:

"And he shewed me a pure river of water of life, clear as crystal, proceeding out of the throne of God and of the Lamb. In the midst of the street of it, and on either side of the river, was there the tree of life, which bare twelve manner of fruits, and yielded her fruit every month: and the leaves of the tree were for the healing of the nations."

The judgment ends with the invitation of Christ as Judge and Redeemer: "Come, ye blessed of my Father, inherit the Kingdom prepared for you from the foundation of the world."—Matt. 24:34. Why say expressly *"from the foundation of the world,"* unless it means that the earth was created for their inheritance, and that at last they are to come into full undisturbed possession and into its eternal enjoyment? "Blessed are the meek, for they shall inherit the earth," may have its partial fulfilment in the present Dispensation, but it surely has its higher and eternal fulfilment in a heavenly sense. The meek have never yet "inherited" except in a very limited degree.

As the birthplace of Christ and the saints, as the scene of the joint sufferings of the Redeemer and His redeemed hosts, and as the glorified bodies of Himself and His people are alike related by their constituent elements to earth, what could be more appropriate than that this world itself should be glorified as their eternal dwelling place; and that the globe where was enacted the cross should become the habitation of his throne, the seat of his Kingdom of righteousness, shared and enjoyed by the saints forever and ever?

The New Jerusalem

Now follows the figurative description of "the Holy Jerusalem" with its gates of pearl, its streets of gold as transparent glass, its walls of jasper, and with its "pure river of the water of life, clear as crystal proceeding out of the throne of God and of the Lamb." The beauty and glory of the celestial city is, however, not its chief attraction, being exceeded by the privileges and blessedness of its inhabitants:

"And there shall be no more curse: but the throne of God and of the Lamb shall be in it; and his servants shall serve him: and they shall see his face; and his name shall be in their foreheads. And there shall be no night there; and they need no candle, neither light of the sun; for the Lord God giveth them light: and they shall reign forever and ever."

Is this description of the New Jerusalem applicable to the present spiritual glory and beauty of the ideal church, the Lamb's wife: or does it symbolize the future blessed state of the righteous in what is commonly known as heaven, the eternal dwelling place of the saints? Possibly it has a dual significance and a twofold fulfilment as in the case of many other prophecies.

Referring again to the illustration of a distant mountain range, which seems one and indivisible, but which afterward proves to be separated into its constituent parts with vast intervening space between, the same is true often of great prophetic future events. Reading the 24th chapter of Matthew, Christ's own answer to the question as to the end of the age and his Second Coming, it is often impossible to determine accurately what applies to His "Coming in His Kingdom" at the close of the Jewish Dispensation, and what has reference to His Second Coming at the end of the Christian Dispensation. They seem like one inseparable distant mountain range; but the first event having already taken place becomes the type and prophecy of the Second.

In all the ages Jerusalem has been used as a dual type of the church. It has been employed as a spiritual name of the church on earth, "Zion, city of our God." It is equally the symbol of heaven, the "city that hath foundations whose builder and maker is God." In like manner the New Jerusalem has the same dual significance. Parts of the description seem applicable exclusively to the present glory of the church, as for example, when it is said "The kings of the earth do bring their glory and honor into it"; and "the leaves of the tree were for the healing of the nations." Other parts are applicable solely to the heavenly Jerusalem, as for example:

"And I saw no temple therein: for the Lord God Almighty and the Lamb are the temple of it. And the city had no need of the sun, neither of the moon, to shine in it; for the glory of God did lighten it, and the Lamb is the light theroef. . . . And there shall be no more curse; but the throne of God and of the Lamb shall be in it; and his servants shall serve him: and they shall see his face; and his name shall be in their foreheads. And there shall be no night there; and they need no candle, neither light of the sun; for the Lord God giveth them light: and they shall reign forever and ever."

THE EPILOGUE

As Christ had spoken the Prologue in the first chapter, it is eminently appropriate that He should close with the Epilogue, which consists of several elements:

1—The Eternity of Destiny

"He that is unjust, let him be unjust still: and he which is filthy, let him be filthy still: and he that is righteous, let him be righteous still: and he that is holy, let him be holy still."

Immutable character makes eternal destiny. The mutable has forever past. It is the age of the immutable—endless as Eternity.

2—The Last Invitation

The Drama of Christianity is about to close. Who but He should speak that closing word? What shall constitute Christ's last message to a lost world? Is not the great invitation characteristic of the God-man, who would make his last message an appeal, the expression of his divine love and of his human sympathy?

Standing in Alpine valleys the guide often sounds a bugle note, and the tourist hears quickly from some near mountain side the resounding echo. Then later the same note at various intervals reverbrates till at last far down the valley, faintly but perfectly distinct, comes back the last lingering echo. In like manner the invitation had sounded and resounded, echoed and re-echoed by prophet and apostle. First came the clear note of Isaiah, the evangelist of the Old Testament: "Ho, every one that thirsteth, come ye to the waters, and he that hath no money, come ye, buy and eat; yea, come, buy wine and milk without money and without price." This was echoed in the call of the Master in His earthly ministry: "In the last day, that great day of the feast, Jesus stood and cried, saying, If any man thirst, let him come unto me, and drink."

Now, sixty years after the Ascension, the echo comes reverberating from heaven itself, the last message of the risen and glorified Christ: "And the Spirit and the bride say, Come. And let him that heareth say, Come. And let him that is athirst come. And whosoever will, let him take the water of life freely." "The Bride," the church, in its divine Word and human ministry extending the outward call, "the Spirit" in the depth of the human soul uttering the inward and effectual call, constitute a united appeal to come to the fountain of life. Lest, however, the Bride should negelect some soul or grow lukewarm in her ministrations, Christ commissions each individual believer to sound the personal invitation—"Let him that heareth, say, Come." If no invitation is given by church or individual, Christ makes the soul's own inherent need and soul-thirst the warrant—"Let him that is athirst come." Then lest any soul fail to recognize the cry of its own unsatisfied nature, he enlarges the invitation till in its mighty sweep it takes in the last living soul and cries, "Whosoever will, let him take the water of life freely." This is not some apostle or lesser herald of the cross. It is Christ Himself calling from the throne, "Come, come, come—whosoever will."

The invitation dies away. The last message has been spoken. That voice will be heard on earth no more by human ears. Never again will the Master plead in person, and never again will He extend the gracious invitation of divine love.

3—The Announcement of His Coming

The message ends with a promise, repeated, echoed all through Revelation: "Behold, I come quickly." John, the last living representative of the Apostles, the last inspired herald of Christ and of the church, voices the feelings, aspirations, and supreme prayer of the saints throughout the ages: "Even so, Come, Lord Jesus."

The curtain rises and falls no more.

The Drama is ended.

It Is Eternity!

INDEX